This book is dedicated to my beautiful wife, Marie, whose bravery, support, strength and unconditional love has been a constant inspiration to me and helps me to carry on.
It appears there is a light at the end of the tunnel.

As Shakespeare said,

To me, fair friend, you never can be old,
For as you were when first your eye I eyed,
Such seems your beauty still.

Though I look old, yet I am strong and lusty;
For in my youth I never did apply
Hot and rebellious liquors in my blood,
Nor did not with unbashful forehead woo
The means of weakness and debility;
Therefore my age is as a lusty winter,
Frosty, but kindly.

As You Like It: William Shakespeare
Yeah, right!

A Light at the End

By
Bryon Williams

A Theatrical Memoir

Copyright © 2019 Bryon Williams

ISBN 978-0-6484238-1-2

Bryon Williams has asserted his right under the Copyright, Designs and Patents Act 1988 to be identified as the author of this work. The information in this book is based on the author's experiences and opinions. Permission to use information has been sought by the author. Any breaches will be rectified in further editions of the book.

All rights reserved. No part of this publication may be reproduced, stored in or introduced into a retrieval system, or transmitted in any form, or by any means (electronic, mechanical, photocopying, recording or otherwise) without the prior written permission of the author. Any person who does any unauthorised act in relation to this publication may be liable to criminal prosecution and civil claims for damages. Enquiries should be made through the publisher.

Also by the same author

The Twilight Escort Agency
Code Name Millicent
The Tourist from the Light
The Burning Boy
The Reluctant Psychic
The Psychic Spy
Naked Warrior

From the age of fifty I found my life speeding up like a Bullet Train on corroded tracks. I flashed through the stations of Grey Hair Grove, Deafness Town, Failing Eyesight Falls, Denture Downs, Celibate City, Replacement Retreat, Varicose Vale, and almost came off the rails at Grumpy Hollow before reaching Senility Square, on the outskirts of Depression Valley.

Not a trip for the faint hearted.

Chapter 1
2010

To give you a picture of the author as you plough your way through the following chapters, I would like to describe myself as tall, slim, olive skinned, with good muscle definition, glossy dark, wavy hair with a hint of silver 'wisdom strands', sparkling blue eyes with a naughty glint, a distinctive, classical profile and an engaging smile that hints of sexual playfulness.

I would very much like to describe myself as such but that would be a trifle exaggerated. In fact, in 1937, my mother gave birth to an eight-pound nose – with a sinus condition – and the rest of me grew on later. This was not a propitious start.

I do have olive skin and my muscles are well defined – by wrinkles and sagging skin. My wife used to say I have always had the body of David, but I have since discovered she was not referring to Michelangelo's masterpiece, but to David Willhelmstein from number 27, who is eighty-two and suffering from some mysterious wasting disease. My hair is completely faded silver and my blue eyes no longer sparkle, except when I bend over and stand up too quickly, but they are, patriotically, red, white and blue, and the sexual playfulness outplayed itself long ago. What happened to the previous exuberant, fun-filled youth, I have no idea. It was like I had dozed off to sleep somewhere in 1980 and suddenly surfaced in

2008. It was sort of an epiphany, really. I suddenly realised that, in fact, I was still living in the 70s; with the same mind set, behaviour, reasoning, ethics, moral standards and, I'm fairly certain, some of the same wardrobe. Mind you, I suspect in the seventies I was still living in the fifties. I just don't seem to be able to catch up. Forget the X and Y generations; I have now entered the Zzzzzzz Generation.

I remember sitting at home watching ABC television with my wife, Marie, who was disabled down the left side from a disastrous stroke she suffered at the beginning of the new millennium. This suspiciously occurred after a neck operation and not being prescribed any blood-thinning drug to counteract clotting.

She hates euphemisms and especially the word 'disabled'. 'I'm not disabled,' she proclaims indignantly, 'I'm fuckin' crippled.' But she says it beautifully. She used to be a speech teacher in bygone years, with a wonderful mercurial voice and a marvellous laugh, which someone once described as 'laughing in arpeggio'. Unfortunately, her voice and speech tended to flatten out a lot after the stroke but she still said 'Fuck' beautifully, and probably a little more frequently.

I have to talk to her seriously about this loathing of euphemisms. 'Now look,' I say, 'you can't have signs up everywhere saying "Fuckin' Cripple Parking" or "Fuckin' Cripple Toilets", someone's sure to take offence.'

She also hates the euphemism 'indigenous', claiming, according to the Oxford Dictionary, it means 'born or produced naturally in a region; belonging naturally'. In which case she claimed to be indigenous, certainly being produced naturally in Queensland in

1937. I have to forcibly stop her from ticking the indigenous box on Government forms.

Anyway, I digress. A BBC programme came on the screen entitled *Grumpy Old Men*, which consisted of a half a dozen men of a similar 'mature' age to myself, I presumed, having a whinge about all sorts of subjects that really pissed them off in today's world. It turned out these 'Grumpy Old Men' were in fact only in their mid fifties! – mere children in their prime. Unfortunately, they don't have an Australian version of the show as yet but no doubt that will follow in due course as copying overseas programs, even the bad ones, seems to be the accepted norm in this country.

To the amazement of She Who Can't Be Ignored, and even myself, I found myself shouting, very loudly and passionately, 'YES! YES! YES!!!' somewhat in the style of Meg Ryan in *When Harry Met Sally*, and without the exchange of any body fluids. What's happening? I wondered. Could there possibly be other men out there who think the same way as I do? I thought I was totally alone in my discontent – but, apparently not.

Why is this? I asked myself, sinking into my now familiar mood of self-psychoanalysis, i.e. talking to myself. Why do we old buggers feel compelled to whinge about seemingly everything? Probably because we've had years of inactivity and irrelevance to review our philosophy on life, I reasoned with myself (another habit I've fallen into), and we've come to the conclusion we're undoubtedly justified looking at the mess the world is in and anybody younger is obviously drugged to eyeballs, ignorant, naive, stupid and downright wrong. Yes, we have reached the age where cynicism has become reality. No wonder Marie refers to me as *The Grumpy Old Withered of Oz*.

Now it's true that this was an English program and in Australia the Poms have a probably undeserved reputation for whinging, and, like the Americans, they do seem to live on a different planet, but there is one thing we do have in common and that is constantly whinging about perceived injustices. Well, I mean, just think about it.

It's the 18th of February in the year 2000 at 6.30pm. I've just finished mowing the lawn and Marie's preparing dinner. We sit on the back terrace overlooking the park and lake, our favourite spot to enjoy a pre-dinner glass of wine, with the sun setting over the distant hills and the water reflecting the wooded hills of the hinterland. It's so peaceful. Marie is telling me about a friend of ours who has just been visiting her daughter in NSW and in mid-sentence, without any hint of a pause, her voice suddenly changes and sounds like an old vinyl record that has suddenly been switched from 78 RPM to 33, every word slowing down and elongated, low and flat.
    I look at her to see if she is joking.
    'Sorry, what did you just say?'
    Continuing in that same flat awful tone she repeats very slowly, 'I... said... Shirley... just... got... back... from... visiting... Amanda ...'
    'Why are you talking like that?' I ask.
    'Like...what?' she drones.
    I suddenly notice she has slumped to her left and her face has dropped slightly on that side. Christ! I immediately

realise in horror, a stroke! She's having a stroke! I race to the phone and dial 000. In seconds our life as we have known it has come to an end and will never be the same again.

Well, for a start, take our average general health. We seem to spend so much bloody time being encouraged to look after our health and beauty, what with doctors' appointments, blood tests, eye tests, X rays, dentists, physiotherapists, not to mention proctologists and urologists, who like to keep their fingers in everything, so to speak, and dozens of other denizens of the medical profession. I swear there are some weeks when it's difficult to find a spare day to fit in the next medical or dental appointment. And their favourite word is always 'degeneration'.

Everything is degenerating. Now, in our youth we took a certain pride in being called a 'degenerate' but in old age the connotations are somewhat different and frankly insufferable. We're literally 'degenerating' at such a pace that it won't be long before our bodies completely disintegrate and crumble away into dust and extinction. If I wake up in the morning and nothing hurts, I think I died during the night.

Yet our minds and senses are constantly flooded with advice from 'experts' at every page turn and channel switch, on how to live longer and of course happier, more beautiful, and healthier lives. Now let's face it, very few of us, if any, look or feel beautiful after the age of, at tops forty, and it's all downhill from there on in until sixty, and then the acceleration increases at such a pace it's like flying into a black hole in space. And after seventy you don't want to know about it and you can really only make future plans up until tomorrow, if there's going to be one. I'm all for 'pushing the borders' or 'looking outside the envelope', but pushing hurts my back, and no matter how hard I try, it still remains stationary, and 'looking outside the envelope' is all very well, if I can find my fucking reading glasses.

The stores and pharmacies are stuffed with rejuvenating creams and lotions to erase lines and wrinkles, blemishes and age – oops – maturity spots. I need a lotion, cream or pill to take away the crow's feet, wrinkles and blemishes in my brain. Diets and advice are pushed at us by a plethora of gurus who have never even been to India. We're steered in every direction from low fat to high fat, no carbs to high carbs, high protein to low protein, lower your cholesterol and eat fat-absorbing spreads, butter is good for you, take vitamins, don't take vitamins, eat this, don't eat that, consume at least three tons of fruit and vegetables a day, drink wine, don't drink wine and definitely don't smoke no matter how addicted you are, but hey, 'It's really important to stay happy and enjoy yourself in old age,' the psychiatrists extol; 'it's good for your heart.' With so many confusing restrictions, how the hell are we supposed to enjoy ourselves? So throw down a Viagra and screw yourself to death. When ya gunna go, at least go happy. And what about that Age-Defying Makeup for women? The only age-defying makeup that works is putty or taking a soak in formaldehyde.

It also amazes me how dentistry has changed since I was a kid. If you had a toothache in those days they were inclined to rip the bloody lot out and fit you with a set of clackers. I have been through 'Brush your teeth in a circular motion, brush your teeth up and down, brush your teeth horizontally, use a hard brush, use a medium brush, use a soft brush. Brush gently, brush vigorously', which I did for years, causing me to wear a trench in the enamel. And now, as the sun sets on the one-time glistening whities and they loosen in their sockets, I sit in the dentist's waiting room singing the Abba hit 'Denture Queen' while I bid farewell to the days of chomping a tough steak and look forward to a diet of vitamised mush.

The ambulance arrives and I'm in such a state of shock I feel helpless and don't know what to do to help her. I've never seen anyone with a stroke before. My mind can't accept the enormity of what is happening. The attendants are serious and efficient, lifting her onto a stretcher and giving her oxygen. I light a cigarette to ease my nerves and one of the attendants snaps, 'Put that out!' They decide to take her to John Flynn Private Hospital and ask if I want to ride with her.

I automatically think we'll need the car to get back home again. The thought of a prolonged stay in hospital never occurs to me. She's never been taken to hospital in an ambulance before. How strange. 'No, I'll follow in the car,' I tell them.

Later she told me she was cold and lonely in the ambulance and she'd thought that I was sending her away to get rid of her. How could she even think I would want to do that? She had no idea what had happened to her.

And of course at this stage, wouldn't you know, Willie, my local member for fun, is no longer a 'standing' member. After dominating my life since I was fourteen or so, he has apparently decided to retire from the house and indeed the party. No more the night-long sessions, the sometimes-bawdy behaviour, the jocular intercourse.

(Or even serious, if it comes to that.) Well, at least I outlived the wrinkly old bastard.

But those of us Withereds in a similar condition are still constantly inundated with images of sex; in fashion, movies, books, mind-numbing celebrity magazines, stage shows, and awful television commercials assuring us that if we buy this or wear that or drive this car, we will become one of the 'beautiful' people and more sexually alluring. Now I'm sorry but can you honestly show me a beautiful, sexually alluring person at seventy?

So if I can no longer get it up does it mean I can't really wear those clothes, drive that car, use that cologne, eat that chocolate, or drink that Coke or expensive wine, because it will make me too sexy, too attractive? Would that be a kind of false advertising on my part? Could I be sued for making myself so sexually alluring that I'm irresistible, and then bomb out at the point of entry, so to speak? In these days of American-inspired lawsuits, probably.

Our son, Ben, arrives at the hospital and it is obvious he is as shocked as I am. We speak little as we sit alone outside the emergency reception and wait, each lost in our own fears. Eventually they call us in and we creep into the emergency ward and find her apparently sleeping. A lady doctor comes up to us and, in reply to our whispered questions, tells us that they're going to admit her into the hospital and no, they can't tell us the extent of the damage until further tests are made but she encourages us to try to keep our hopes up because some stroke victims recover fairly quickly. She doesn't.

And speaking of lawsuits, why is it that there always has to be someone to blame, to sue, for the slings and arrows of outrageous fortune? What happened to personal responsibility? If you trip over a crack in the road or fall into a manhole someone has left open, don't sue, open your fucking eyes.

I really think, though, that there should be a different set of laws, rules and regulations for the over sixties. I mean, we were brought up in a different era with different attitudes, different standards. It's like the Western civilisations trying to understand the Orientals, or Middle Eastern cultures, or men trying to understand women. We don't THINK the same! Idiocy in laws, rules and regulations has existed in every era to cater for the lowest common denominator and the intellectually challenged. Well, we're not *all* intellectually challenged and as you get older you have more experience and time to think and object to intrusive laws and see them for the insults and manipulation of power many of them really are. Warn us of the dangers by all means and then, as long as it doesn't hurt anyone else, let us make up our own bloody minds but don't make it a law.

Seat belts for instance; now personally I agree with wearing them; it makes sense to me. But if someone doesn't want to wear one, let them kill themselves running into a tree as long as they don't kill others or damage the tree. And if the beneficiaries complain and threaten to sue, the courts could say, 'Sorry, they were warned. Next case!'

The same could be said for smoking. Now don't start me on that.

The tests prove she's had a massive stroke. She is completely paralysed down her left side and if she recovers there is a doubt that she will ever walk or function normally again. The implications are horrendous. On the way home I do a lot of thinking. I think about how much she means to me; the history we have shared. The way she has cared for me during the forty years of our marriage, forgoing her own career for the sake of mine, supporting me and our small son when I was out of work, spoiling us, loving us unconditionally. I make a solemn commitment to look after her and care for her for as long as I am able, 'till death us do part', as we vowed in our wedding ceremony, to give her the most comfortable and happiest life I can.

Chapter 2

Oh, alright then. I have been a dedicated smoker for sixty-five years and yes, I am still alive, and yes, I am hopelessly addicted. But I happen to enjoy smoking as much as others enjoy alcohol or playing pool or sport or knitting. In the fifties it was almost obligatory to smoke. And in the forties the Red Cross and other charities packed cartons of cigarettes and tobacco in food parcels to the soldiers in the front lines. But then again, that was before paranoia set in, backed by yet more 'scientific experts'.

The non-smoking fraternity who had been unjustly forced to put up with nasty, smelly smokers for years were ecstatic. At last they had a cause, a justification for their distaste. Once they got their noses out of the clouds of smoke there was simply no stopping them. And the reformed smokers who joined them became even worse. 'If we can give it up, so should you and to help you we'll find some other experts to agree with us on passive smoking, and hire spin doctors to really lay it on thick and frighten the shit out of you.' And they did.

I have tried to quit many times, mainly because of well-meaning and now consequently ex-friends complaining about my filthy habit, and of the constant rises in cost, which we really can't be seen to complain about as the habit has been made so antisocial by the wowser, non-smoking fraternity you feel obliged to at least appear to be shamefully contrite, weak and miserable to justify your existence. About one in five people smoke. That's still a lot of deviate devotees. It's amazing how quiet we are, considering. And now they're talking about banning electronic cigarettes that don't smell and only emit vapour! Are they going to ban asthma vaporisers?

The last time I tried to give up I was in hospital recovering from my third hip replacement operation. (I do think three hip replacements for a biped a little extreme but there you go.) Before I was put into Home Transitional Care, I was transferred into what I thought was to be a rehabilitation establishment, which turned out to be in an old people's nursing home. This was my first experience in this type of institution and it shattered me to the core of my being. I had to share my room with a lovely old bloke who was recovering from a recent stroke, which of course was a constant reminder of my wife's experience, and he liked to have his radio on from wake-up to pass-out time and we weren't supplied with headphones. Now I don't mind the radio, but constant talk-back programs? Sharing my bed with Alan Jones is not one of my secret lusts.

The rest of the inmates were incredibly sad with the majority bedridden and many lying around all day like cast-offs in a vegetable patch, with no communication skills left. That is except for one old dear who conversed very loudly in Russian, which is not my strongest language, and which didn't deter her in the least. If it was a prerequisite for all politicians before entering Parliament to spend a month in a nursing home, a bill in favour of euthanasia would be passed quicker than their next pay rise. Thankfully there are a few caring doctors out there who are willing to risk their careers to ease the suffering of the terminally ill with ever-increasing lethal doses of morphine.

So I escaped out into a small garden, just outside the dining area, and there to my delighted astonishment, was an ashtray! There is a God, I thought. Obviously, if he wanted me to stop smoking, he wouldn't have left that ashtray in the exact position where I was sitting. I remember having two quick consecutive thoughts:
1. I've got to get back to my cell and find my fags! (Which I'd hidden in my suitcase out of temptation's way); and
2. Get me the hell outta this place!

I'd lasted six days and on the seventh day I rested, with a beautiful fag. So endeth the lesson.

She survives the stroke but many of her motor skills have been lost and she is transferred to a private room. She can communicate with difficulty but the paralysis remains. I visit the hospital daily and when friends arrive we all try to stay jolly. It's hard, so hard seeing her lying there, for all of us who remember how vibrant and vivacious she was just a few days before.

'And she can even brush her own teeth now,' I proudly announce, to ease a lull in the awkward conversation.

'Darling, you make me sound like an idiot,' comes the low drawl from the bed.

I must be so careful what I say. This is all so new to me.

All the men in my family smoked and yes, they all eventually died. Funny that, but as far as I know, none of them died from a smoking-related disease. Mind you, nowadays no matter what you die of, if they find out you were or had ever been a smoker, you immediately join the statistics of Smoking-Related Deaths. I suspect if you get run over by a drugged-up lorry driver when you're having a nice quiet fag waiting outside a shop, at of course the obligatory four metres from the entrance, it would immediately be included in the Smoking-Related Death stats. Naturally, the lorry driver wouldn't be included in the tobacco-related death stats, unless of course he was a smoker as well as a druggie.

We can't even have an enjoyable smoke with a cup of coffee at an outside cafe where the pollution from passing traffic is so bad you need a good drag to take away the taste of the exhaust fumes, which I am sure are much healthier. I must say, you meet a much nicer class of people sitting on the kerb outside buildings having a fag. They seem less stressed and more friendly; a sort of club. Of course, you can't sit in a chair and look too comfortable. You must look as degraded and desperate as possible.

And yet, and this must be kept in strictest confidence, I have discovered a licensed restaurant where you can actually sit at a table in the designated area on a pleasant terrace, and have a cup of coffee or a glass of booze and smoke! The smoking area abuts several other unlicensed cafes, which do not allow smoking! It must be no more than a metre away from the no-smoking area of the next-door cafe. Very sensible law, I'm sure. Go figure. But of course they're now talking about stopping smoking even outside shopping malls so there goes another bastion of pleasure.

> *She's been transferred to another hospital for rehabilitation and there is some improvement. I visit at least twice daily and spend as much free time with her as I can when I'm not working. My heart breaks each time I see her but I try not to show it. Slowly she regains some mobility*

but there is only limited left leg movement and no movement in her left arm at all. She's wheelchair-bound of course and they've fitted her with a plastic leg brace because she has a 'dropped foot condition' with no ankle control, but she still tries to keep up with the various exercises. They manage to get her into the hydrotherapy pool each morning and she can walk around the pool, hanging onto the bar and exercise without the brace.

She even manages to put on a little makeup as long as someone opens the various bottles and jars for her. The male patients are only too willing to help her with that. She's always had a way with men. Amazingly she's keeps up her spirits and tries to jolly along the other patients. How does she do it?

We were in Italy in 1999 and I remember going into a restaurant which didn't have outside tables, and I said to the manager, 'I suppose all the tables inside are non-smoking?' He looked at me with a slightly puzzled expression and said, 'No, but I think there's a non-smoking table down the back near the toilets.' Everyone seemed to be smoking just about anywhere, even the manager and the chef. We almost decided to immigrate. We returned in 2008 and much had changed; you could still smoke in many restaurants and *trattorias* but only outside, which I thought was fair enough.

We don't want to offend anyone. We don't want to blow our smoke into the faces of the scowling opposition regardless of whether they have communicable diseases, halitosis, body odour or they're just plain ugly and unfriendly. Just give us a pleasant, civilised, separate area to relax and smoke in and if it offends you, or you're paranoid about smoking, piss off! We won't interfere with you if you don't interfere with us.

And don't talk to me about the cost of smoking-related illnesses. With the millions of dollars smokers pay in taxes surely we've paid enough to warrant care or at least a lethal injection to put us out of our misery. That way we'd be able to free up more hospital beds for the really needy cases like obesity, which takes up one hospital bed in six, sclerosis of the liver from alcohol poisoning, or drug overdose or gunshot patients, or speeding drunk drivers, or domestic violence wounds. We keep being told that the world is over-populated and we're constantly short of hospital beds and yet they keep coming up with new ways to keep us living longer. Why?

I notice all hotel rooms and apartments and even tourist caravan and camping parks have banned smoking. They don't stipulate 'No drugs or alcohol and definitely no sniffing cocaine, or shooting up heroin', so I suppose that's acceptable, and do those signs on the lawns really mean 'Keep off the grass', or am I being paranoid? No smoking indoors I can understand, but outside? And old addicted pensioners who have been smoking for over twenty years and are still alive should be given a card to allow them to get their ciggies tax-free. I read the other day in *National Geographic* that if you give up smoking for ten years, you have a fifty percent chance of not contracting lung cancer or having a heart attack. Super odds for a 'degenerating', seventy-year-old, fifty-five-year smoker! If it wasn't for tobacco crops the early settlers in America would never have survived as it was their major, if not only export crop. Early America was built on tobacco sales.

Get a phone call from the hospital while I'm at work. 'Sorry to bother you, Mr Williams, but we have to let you know that your wife is fine but she had a bit of an accident this morning and hit her head when she fell off the toilet. The trainee nurse unfortunately left her by herself for a minute. The nurse has been reprimanded. There was no real damage.'

I think I overreacted.

And speaking of drugs, why does it always seem to be the young folk getting busted? It's us old Withereds who really need the drugs, for God's sake. Up to the local chemist, flash your pension card and pick up half a kilo of cocaine. They could colour it pink and if you're caught selling it you lose your pension. As a matter of fact you should be able to get other essentials tax free or rebated on your pension card; like petrol and alcohol, food and clothes, Viagra or Cialis or those Caverject injections you stick in your dick. Don't give us extra pension money; we'll only give it to our kids. Give us lots of rebates.

She spent her childhood in Cairns and reminisces often about how she loved school and the many multicultural friends she made. The memory of being tied up to the rotary clothesline to stop her from constantly wandering or being hit by a train on the nearby railway track frustrated her however, but she was proud of the time her older brother was attacked by a gang of youths who were in the midst of stringing him up from the branch of a tree when she fearlessly stepped in and routed their endeavours and sent them packing in no uncertain terms.

She was never told as a child that her father, Archie, had joined the army and was posted to Milne Bay in New

Guinea where he took part in the historic battle that followed. For the first time, the Australians successfully defeated the relentless Japanese invasion and forced them to retreat. When he finally returned and she discovered the reason for his disappearance, she assumed that as a musician he was only involved in playing in the company band and never saw any action. Like most returned soldiers of the period he never spoke of his experiences and only ever really related to his fellow musicians and war comrades, who remained friends for the rest of their lives. But as I pointed out to her, he was regarded as a crack rifle shot and was probably enlisted as a sniper. Besides, being under mortal siege, it was doubtful he was only occupied playing his clarinet while the Japanese ran riot.

He returned a changed man, unrecognisable from the man who left his five-year-old daughter; tanned and slim and prone to bouts of depression and violence which frightened her and which she never understood. It sounded to me like a classic case of Post-Traumatic Stress Disorder and the effects never entirely disappeared.

She often reminisces about riding her bike to school and avoiding the masses of cane toads and the occasional snake on the roads by lifting her feet up onto the handlebars. She can still recall the smell of coconut oil coming from the hair of the Torres Strait Islander classmates, the marvellous Chinese food cooked by her Yin Foo friends and the incredible Italian food when visiting the local cane farmers and cutters. I think this experience was the reason for her love of cooking of which I was a very willing beneficiary.

Chapter 3

We moved into an 'Over Fifties Resort', which is a bit of a misnomer; I mean there was no room service number on the phone, no restaurant or licensed bar, they don't service the rooms and there's no bikini-clad beauties frolicking around the unheated pool. At best we have a bunch of positively obese bodies or scrawny types with surplus skin and sagging muscles, flapping around in the pool doing aerobics or heart classes. The 'tour desk' or 'caretaker's office' proudly displays brochures for podiatrists and hairdressers and lists of emergency telephone numbers for doctors or therapists. And nobody is under sixty because you wouldn't be seen dead in this sort of place if you were still in your fifties, so why don't they call them Over Sixties Resorts? It's an age perception thing I suppose.

But having said all that, it is the best move we ever made. We live in a very comfortable 'villa', which has nothing to do with the Mediterranean kind, but more what you'd call in the 'olden days', a small detached cottage. We are relatively free of 'young people', thank God, and grandchildren are allowed to visit only if it is entirely essential, and must be kept securely tethered, gagged and on a leash and accompanied at all times.

We're allowed one small pet, which must be constrained within your premises, but otherwise the residents are allowed to roam freely and exercise the pet as long as you pick up your doggie poo.

We have an electric security gate at the front entrance, which I'm not sure if it's to keep would-be rapists and robbers out or to keep us in. Mind you, I think some of the single ladies wouldn't mind the occasional visit from the friendly neighbourhood sex maniac.

The other members of the community are compatible and as we're basically all whingers in varying degrees, we can relate to each other perfectly. You do have to speak loudly and clearly though and repeat yourself often or no one can hear you, but that is a small price to pay for retirement in comfort and solitude amongst one's peers.

I'd love a dollar for every free Government-sponsored hearing aid that's left lying around unused in bedside drawers. The first time I remembered to take my hearing aid to the movies was when we went to see that Mel Gibson's film, *Apocalypto*, which turned out to be completely subtitled! But I could hear the other patrons perfectly, munching their popcorn and rustling their sweets wrappers and farting. Hearing aids give you volume but not necessarily clarity. Or maybe it just seems that way today because most people mumble or speak in funny accents.

She pushes the call button repeatedly as she urgently needs a nurse to help her to the toilet or commode chair. Nobody responds for twenty minutes by which time it is too late. This is not unusual. Commode chairs are in short supply and sometimes I have to frantically rush from ward to ward in search of one, disturbing the other patients as I mutter in frustration and toss furniture around in my search. The indignity of it must be appalling for her. But she appears to accept anything that happens to her without complaint. I don't!

Chapter 4

John, a Withered Englishman and fellow tenant, who is obviously far less tolerant than I, lifted his head from his serving of beef and black bean sauce and special fried rice, scowled, and apropos of nothing in particular, grumbled, 'Bloody Baby Boomers.'

We were sitting around one of the tables in the Community Centre Dining Room, celebrating 'Droolies' Week', which falls fifty years after Schoolies' Week, sharing a Chinese banquet kindly provided by the hard-working ladies of the Resort's Social Club. The room was full of laughter and cheerful camaraderie as usual, and I could hear snippets of lively conversation ranging from the latest National Rugby League ladder positions, to back aches, joint replacements, colonoscopies, mammograms, mastectomies and other mystery maladies, lawn bowls, line dancing and other vitally important subjects of national interest, while Ian was calling out the winners of the meat tray raffle. In other words it was a hive of bonhomie and unparalleled excitement.

I was feeling quite mellow, and well into my second glass of Merlot. It's a favourite of mine, a local cleanskin variety, cheap, with a vintage stretching back to last Tuesday; not so much a cheeky wine, as downright abusive. Cyril, from number 102, was sitting opposite, well into his second bottle of Chardonnay and feeling no pain and She Who Can't Be Ignored was sitting next to me, clacking her chopsticks and giving them a fine workout.

'What was that, John?' I asked over the surrounding chatter.

'Bloody Baby Boomers,' he repeated, raising his normally quiet voice somewhat.

Naturally thinking he was referring to the junior league of the Australian basketball team, and knowing precious little of that particular sport anyway (apart from the players being unnaturally tall and wearing long baggy shorts and oversized singlets, which makes them look like giant, sloppy teenagers or Praying Mantises), I replied somewhat tentatively, 'Yeah – how did the youngsters do this week?'

'Who?' he frowned.

'The young Boomers,' I replied patiently.

'No,' he said, 'not the Boomers, the Bloody *Baby* Boomers!'

'Oh,' I said, 'I didn't know they were into basketball. Wouldn't they be a bit old?'

He took a deep breath and sighed. 'Forget the basketball, I'm talking about the *Bloody Baby Boomers*!' he reiterated loudly. 'The ones responsible for the shit the world is in today.'

'Oh, right.' I politely wiped the remains of the chicken satay from my chin and the front of my shirt, while Cyril opted to forget eating and settle into finishing his second bottle.

John forcefully tapped his finger on the table in front of him to add emphasis to his words. 'The Bloody Baby Boomers completely rejected the values, traditions and morals of their parents and grandparents.' He paused and gave me a piercing look. 'And look what that's led to.'

He obviously was expecting some sort of intelligent response which completely eluded me, so I reached for the one remaining spring roll before anyone else could pinch it. 'Oh yes, bloody baby bloomers,' I chortled, trying to inject a little of my well-known humour into the conversation. 'But now you can buy those plastic-lined models that you don't have to wash – you just throw them out.'

He sighed and raised his voice even further to almost a shout to cater for my occasional lapse of hearing, and slowed his words down like I was some dim-witted Hungarian immigrant just off the boat. 'Boomers, not *bloomers*! The Bloody Baby Boomers!'

'Oh – right. What have they done now?'

'Isn't it obvious?' he asked incredulously. 'The Bloody Baby Boomers were born in the years following the end of the war, right? Now there were obviously a stack of them, what with their fathers away overseas for years and all that. And remember, this was the time before the Pill.'

'But they did have French Letters,' I reminded him.

'I'm not talking about the bloody French,' he replied dismissively.

'Condoms,' I translated for him.

'I was born there,' piped up Cyril.

'You were born in a condom?' I asked incredulously.

'No,' said Cyril derisively, 'Condong – northern New South Wales.'

'And the Pope did advocate abstinence and the Rhythm Method,' Anthea spoke up from the other end of the table.

'Yeah, but a lot of couples were horny and bonking to the wrong beat,' John shot back at her.

Anthea retreated into her chicken and sweet corn soup.

'So,' John continued unabashed, 'when the troops came home from the war there was a lot of fu–' he stopped in deference to Anthea '– hanky-panky going on. And the result was a whole heap of babies. When they were born, the new Mums and Dads went berserk and indulged the little darlings outrageously. And as the kids grew up, the parents naturally wanted to make sure the precious little offspring had a better life than they or their parents had, what with the Great Depression and …'

'My Dad humped his bluey during the Great Depression,' Cyril butted in.

John was obviously not aware that the term 'humping yer bluey' referred to carrying a blanket roll stuffed with your belongings on your back, and had nothing remotely to do with having deviant sexual relations with your red-headed mate.

'What, he was a homo?' John exclaimed.

'No!' retorted the outraged Cyril. 'He was a hobo, not a homo.'

This slice of Australiana was obviously far too confusing for an Englishman to digest, so after a suspicious glance at Cyril, John continued. 'But the bloody parents completely forgot that struggle creates character. Look how us Brits rallied during the Blitz.'

'Yeah, you were bloody marvellous,' I mumbled through a mouthful of Chinese delicacy. 'My Gran used to send you food parcels. Did you ever get them?'

'What?' John shook his head, somewhat baffled.

'Gran's food parcels, did you ever get them?'

A puzzled expression crept over John's countenance for a moment, before he shook his head and finally muttered, 'Yeah, thank her for me.'

'Too late, mate, she died in '57.'

'And then with the post-war economic boom,' John persisted, 'and the new technological advances fuelling consumer demand …' he'd obviously read that somewhere '… the parents pushed, encouraged and swamped their kids with material values and higher education and expectations. They spoiled them rotten and of course, the bloody kids took it all for granted, as kids do.'

Now I am well known for my equanimity and reluctance to encourage disputation, so I tried to diffuse the situation with simple logic. 'So, what you're saying is that it was the parents of the Bloody Baby Boomers who were really to blame?' I said reaching for another spoonful of sweet and sour and hoping to bring the tirade to a hasty conclusion.

'No.' John recoiled in indignation at the suggestion. 'The parents were being kind and thoughtful, but the Bloody Baby Boomers were just ungrateful little sods.'

'Well, I'll be buggered,' I moaned, realising I'd missed the last of the dim sims, which She Who Can't Be Ignored had snaffled.

'Right, and so we all are,' he agreed, 'because, as a result of the returning Diggers' indulgence, they innocently created the bloody Me Generation that eventually turned into the Bloody Baby Boomers Generation, and now, God help us, *they've* produced the bloody X and Y Generations.'

'That's what we call the Generation Gap, John, in fact there seem to be several generation gaps in your argument,' I struggled, trying to keep abreast of his logic.

'This is not a gap, this is a fu–' another sideward glance at Anthea, '– bloomin' chasm!'

'An' wha' abou' those young hoons that sit on ya bumper an' tailgate ya on the motorway?' Cyril suddenly threw into the conversation out of the blue.

'Now, they're just mongrels.' I quickly tried to adapt to this new twist in the repartee and encourage a more positive line of debate.

'And did the Bloody Baby Boomers really appreciate it?' John demanded, determined not to be distracted from his train of thought. 'No. They went mad and took the hard-earned and misplaced generosity of their parents, as if it was their God-given right. And in the process, the Bloody Baby Boomers lost any essence of compassion, sense of community, and duty of care for their elders and children and of their fellow man,' he expounded decisively with a fist slam on the table that rattled the bowls, and drew scowls of indignation from Anthea.

'An' they speed up an' pass ya, an' cut in front of ya, an' almost run ya off the road. Some of 'em just young slips of girls too,' Cyril cut in, away on his own train of thought which I seriously doubted would ever pull in to a station. 'Bloody women drivers,' he muttered.

I leaned back in my chair, delicately sipped my wine and waited, realising at this stage there was no stopping the confusing tirade of conversation.

'The Bloody Baby Boomers,' John continued, refusing to be distracted, 'were so busy amassing wealth, position, material gain and physical comfort, they didn't have the time or the ability to instil the basic qualities of common decency and work ethics into their offspring. Greed became a virtue, if not an art form. Madonna's "Material Girl" became their bloody anthem.'

'Bloody Catholics,' Cyril retorted with a slight slur.

That stopped John in his tracks for a second. He squinted at Cyril with a puzzled look and said, 'What's it got to do with Catholics?'

'The Madonna.' Cyril belched discreetly. 'You said something about the Madonna. Wasn't she a Catholic?'

'I'm a Catholic,' piped up Anthea from the other end of the table, in what could only be described as a warning tone. Anthea had unfortunately lost her husband a few years back, and never found him again. There was a suspicion he fled to Vanuatu. 'And Liberal,' she added ominously, thus putting an end to any further meaningful discussion on Religion or Politics. But just in case I was tempted, She Who Can't Be Ignored prodded me with her walking stick as a warning.

'Aren't they all,' muttered Cyril, a Protestant and a fierce Labor supporter.

John sighed and relentlessly resisted any attempt to sidetrack him from his perilous course.

'And now the Bloody Baby Boomers' kids are outdoing their parents with even bigger houses with bigger mortgages that they can't afford, cars for every member of the family, boats, clothes that are thrown out before they wear out, electronic gadgets that numb their brains, and God knows what else. And they wouldn't dream of saving enough money to pay for all this crap, they take out loans or put it on their credit cards, and then have the nerve to complain about the bloody interest rates! And the less fortunate of their addled offspring fall behind and are unable to cope or compete, and turn to drugs and alcohol to escape from their parents or their peer group pressure, and then they turn to violence and crime to support their addictions. And the bloody Government will even pay them to leave home!'

Cyril nodded wisely. 'And then they become Rock musicians.'

John decided rightly to ignore Cyril's interjection. 'And now, the basic necessities of life – food, water, shelter, health, education and love – are fast becoming out of reach for the less fortunate, neglected, or brain damaged,' he continued relentlessly. 'For God's sake, there's enough wealth and technological ability available in the world to do away with poverty and neglect but the greedy multinationals, corrupt businessmen, financial institutions and politicians are only interested in the bottom line and holding onto their cushy positions with their monstrous salaries, pensions and bonuses, and the poor people and the disadvantaged can all get stuffed!'

'And the pensioners,' Cyril added helpfully. 'We're always stuffed.'

'So what do the Bloody Baby Boomers' kids do?' John almost snarled, again ignoring Cyril's uninvited contribution. 'The mothers go out to work and leave the kids to fend for themselves and rave on about the cost of child care and the couple of hours of "quality time" they give them, which amounts to social media bullying, endless bloody video games, a couple of hours in front of the telly, or they put them into child care which they can't afford, imagining that will replace discipline and a good steady home life. And now they want bloody paid maternity leave! If you can't afford to have a kid and look after it, don't bloody well have one! The parents have to take on extra jobs to pay for the ever-mounting bills, and everybody's so busy trying to keep up with everybody else, they've stopped talking to the neighbours, or to each other.'

I did think John was being a trifle harsh, and I am not one to interfere in a man's right to his opinion, but by now the food and wine had really kicked in and I could tell the time for Cyril's afternoon nap was fast approaching. His eyelids began to droop and he tried to hold them back up with his arthritic fingers, as John leaned forward and said earnestly, 'Is it really necessary to have more than one modest-sized home? Do they really need huge, multiple rooms, fitted with all the latest furniture, fittings and mod cons, swimming pools, expensive landscaping, more than one car, a boat, flat-screen televisions and computers in every room, bloody video games, iPods or other useless electronic gadgets?'

I opened my mouth to answer but he ploughed on unremittingly. Cyril dropped his eyelids in favour of grabbing his bottle and, draining the remains into his glass, took a final slug of wine and gave another, not so discreet, belch.

'Does all this so-called prosperity bring contentment and happiness and inner peace? Does it make a family? I don't fuckin' think so.'

There was a strangled cry of horror from Anthea's end of the table at the sound of the infamous four-letter word.

John's voice lowered, in deference to Anthea, his forces, one hoped, apparently spent, and there was a thoughtful pause as I nodded wisely in what I hoped looked like universal agreement and understanding. Anthea readied herself to leave, the conversation obviously becoming a little too forceful for her. She carefully screwed the top back on her water bottle, neatly folded her paper napkin and replaced it in her handbag for later.

Cyril began to nod.

'It's become a never-ending circle,' John said, hopelessly. 'Maybe that's why the young people of today are so obese and unfit and wear sloppy clothes that make them look like destitute street kids with their bum cracks showing. You never see them smile or laugh much, except at something that's bad-mannered, insulting or vulgar.'

He shook his head in consternation.

Maybe that's why they don't show any respect for their parents, us older people, or authority.' He paused again in soulful retrospection and shrugged, which was difficult with his shoulder dislocation from lawn bowls. 'Maybe it's well deserved. Maybe they're rejecting the standards that have been forced on them by the Bloody Baby Boomers, who stupidly thought they were doing the right thing. And maybe, in their own fashion their kids are searching for a better and less pretentious way for themselves and the world. I hope they find it soon without doing too much damage in the process and forcing the Government to cut the pension.'

At the mention of the word 'pension', Cyril stirred restlessly but was unable to contribute anything more than a nod.

Anthea stood up, alarmingly agile for her age and hip replacement, and drawing her dignity up to her full five feet two inches, announced scathingly to John and the rest of the table, 'I'm a Baby Boomer, you silly old fart, and proud of it. You think it's been easy for us? Every generation rebels and every generation has its own set of problems and we all have to try to be compassionate and tolerant as we age but that obviously isn't in everybody's nature,' she said rather pointedly. 'One of the major problems of being a Baby Boomer is having to put up with grumpy, miserable old men who never stop complaining about anyone under seventy and expect everyone else to think as they do.'

She paused for effect like an actress about to make her grand final exit. 'And now it's time for my pedicure.' And with that she swept from the room.

For once John was speechless at what he considered this uncalled-for counter-attack.

'Bloody Baby Boomers,' Cyril mumbled, as his head finally dropped forward onto his chest, his breathing becoming a gentle snore. I glanced at She Who Can't Be Ignored and noticed that she too had dropped off.

'You know, John,' I said, finally managing to throw my own inimitable words of wisdom into the arena, 'I think we're all getting a bit too old for this shit. Cyril and my little love blossom here have got the right idea. Let's have another glass of wine and go home for our nanny naps before it's time to listen to the BBC Overseas News Broadcast on the wireless and see what Hitler's up to.'

There's no better sport for an Aussie than taking the piss out of a Pom.

The change is incredibly difficult to accept. This is outwardly not the same woman I married. Got to get used to it and adapt. Many of her motor skills seem to have been rewired. She doesn't recognise her left arm or leg and they are unable to respond to her commands. There is very little expression in her face; not because she doesn't feel it inside, but the muscles just won't work that way. If she is emotionally moved by something on television, or something sad that happens to someone, the tears simply roll gently down her cheeks.

It takes two years before she can smile and that was the result of a tasteless dirty joke I cracked. Looks like I've got to get used to talking dirty which will be so difficult for me. She was always smiling and laughing. Her voice remains flat and inexpressive where before it was so alive and mercurial. In eight years she has not laughed. At most I might get a little twisted smile and a sort of grunt. She can tell me if she thinks something is funny but she just can't express it. For someone who was so vital and expressive it is so heartbreaking and almost unbearable.

The way we were.

Engagement

Wedding at St John's Cathedral

After the ceremony. All dolled up for 'Going Away'.

The Caretaker with Brian Moll

Cat on a Hot Tin Roof with Alan Denby

Seductive in drag for *Charley's Aunt*

Wonderful as Eliza Doolittle in *Pygmalion*

A young Marie as Sabrina in *Sabrina Fair*. No, that's not me with her. I think I was still in school.

Chapter 5

Speaking of the pet we're allowed at the Resort, we have a cat called Rocky. He's a Short-haired Oriental with a pedigree that befits his nature; aloof and disdainful and at times thoroughly unlikable. His pedigree name is Medici Crocodile Hunter, would you believe, but we don't call him that. Can you imagine screaming that out when his gourmet dinner is ready? Not that he comes then anyway. He's a cat!

We have a love/hate relationship; he loves me and I hate him most of the time. The main problem is we are both control freaks and other cat owners will understand the ramifications of that problem. There can only be one boss and he's determined it will be him and he berates me constantly in a voice similar to the sound of a Tasmanian Devil on heat. As resort regulations demand, he must be restrained within the villa confines and we have to provide a cat litter tray for his considerable amount of excretions. As these occur incredibly frequently and as he refuses to use a 'soiled tray', as he puts it, it is my duty to dispose of the results of the said bladder and bowel movements constantly, otherwise he relieves himself in and around the laundry drain hole and then screams for me to clean it up.

I must say that one of the most invaluable advances in technology of this modern age is the discovery of clumping cat litter. Before I discovered this wonder of technology, it was costing me a fortune in cat litter. I was getting it delivered in five-ton truckload quantities. Now, with the aid of a surgical oxygen mask, I can scoop up the clumps with a large shovel and stagger to the wheelie bin.

When we lived in our previous home he was allowed to be an 'outside cat' and loved roaming around freely with the grass between his toes, terrorising the wildlife and playing 'catch me if you can' with the local greyhound. But now, at the Resort, he's not allowed those privileges and is kept incarcerated inside with only a grumpy old pensioner and his disabled wife for company. Well, that is, most of the time. He spends many hours patrolling the windows and doors to see if per chance I have inadvertently left one open, which occasionally happens. Ya gotta be quick.

I arrive early to have lunch with her and unbeknown to her, I stand at the back of the rehab room watching her work. She's standing, supported by side rails! My heart leaps and tears flood my eyes as she determinedly attempts to walk; very unsteadily she manages a few awkward steps.
    Dear God, she'll walk again!
    She looks up and notices me and actually smiles in triumph.

If he manages to 'fly the coop', he's gone and no amount of coaxing, cajoling, threatening or calling will get him back until he's ready. I think he, like me, has a bad case of selective hearing. He immediately sets off, squirting the entire compound to reinstate his territory, which some of the non-cat-loving residents tend to object to for some reason. Immediately he escapes I have to ring all the residents that are prone to object and say, 'Guard yourself, the

Monster's loose!' I'm thinking of installing a 'Rocky Siren'. Mind you, there are a few strays that invade the place from time to time and I'm sure he gets blamed for their squirts. Isn't that like Life? We're always getting blamed for other people's 'squirts'.

I eventually bought a cat harness. That'll teach the little bastard, I thought. Now he can join us for breakfast on the back deck, tethered to the leg of a heavy cane armchair, and we can eat in peace without the excruciating background sound effects of a screaming mongrel cat, locked inside, demanding to join us.

The first morning was a great success and he took to the harness remarkably well, rolling in the warm sun and purring contentedly. Success at last, I thought.

On the second morning, I misjudged the length of line I'd let out on the harness. Whilst I was occupied, running back and forth between the kitchen and the deck, as is usual, serving She Who Can't Be Ignored's breakfast (we couldn't afford a tray), Mongrel Cat managed to drag the half-ton cane chair a few extra feet and, as was his previous habit, jumped through the bars of the railing to escape to the garden about ten feet below. He, the harness and restraining cord, with a fast-following cane chair attached, plummeted through the air for about three feet and came to a sudden stop, when the said chair refused to squeeze through the bars of the railing. No doubt in shock from this suddenly interrupted descent, he found himself swinging gently in the breeze, several feet above the ground, and to all appearances, quite enjoying the view and the experience.

Quickly I dived for the restraining cord and grabbed it to pull him back up. It was a bit like landing a good-sized snapper. But the extra strain this caused made the clip on the harness snap open and he dropped to the ground and landed, looking somewhat stunned, I admit, and with a final sneer of disdain and triumph, sauntered off into the underbrush. He did not return for several hours, during which time I hit the phone warning all the neighbours, 'Arm yourselves and lock the doors, the Monster's loose!'

When the monster from hell eventually carks it, and that could be sooner than he thinks, I think I'll get a lovely dog. Dogs have owners, cats have staff.

I arrive for a visit and find her reading a magazine. She's always been an avid reader but has shown no interest since being in hospital. This is great, I think, she's able to read again. Then I notice the magazine is upside down.

Chapter 6

Apart from the Clumping Cat Litter there are other technological advances that do not have the same appeal. Take computers for example. Now I identify a lot with my computer. I started off with lots of drive and memory, then I became outdated and hopelessly frustrating and annoying, and eventually I had to get my parts replaced. Hopefully when I suffer the last crash I'll have enough power left to hit the delete key. I have also entertained the thought of logging off with a twelve-gauge shotgun. I have now fitted an airbag to my keyboard in case I fall asleep while I'm reading my emails.

Like many of my contemporaries I resisted using a computer for many years until a so-called, and now consequently an ex friend of mine, misguidedly convinced me to upgrade into the twentieth century. I purchased the very latest model for that week and made my first mistake: I brought it home. I studied the manual for hours – something I am not renowned for doing with other appliances – trying to make some sense of it, until in gibbering frustration, I threw it away and got on with it, using my own innate intuition to master the brute.

Now, when it comes to technical manuals, I normally have a photographic memory but it seems I've run out of film or my battery's going flat. After several more hours of mind-blowing frustration, I picked up the phone and called the supplier. Before he had time to say, 'Good afternoon, this is Simon, how can I help you?' I was delivering a vicious tirade about the stupidity of fuckin' computers and spluttering, 'All I wanted was something that I could write a few words with, on a machine that did what I told it to do, and I don't need all of the other crap this product from another galaxy is offering me, and I don't need a three-and-a-half-inch floppy because I already have one and my memory stick has lost its memory!'

There was a long pause, while no doubt poor Simon was waiting for me to draw breath, and then he said, rather patronisingly I thought, 'Well sir, you can return it of course, or may I suggest you perhaps purchase an electric typewriter, or if that is also too difficult for you, may I suggest perhaps a ballpoint pen, or we now have the very latest in lead pencils.'

I was staggered at this effrontery and insult to my intelligence, which gave me pause, before taking a deep controlled breath into my lower intercostal diaphragmatic lung area and with as much dignity as I could manage, muttered through gritted teeth, 'Thank you, patronising young person,' and hung up.

How dare that young whipper-snapper insinuate that I'm stupid, I thought. I'll lick this fuckin' machine if it's the last thing I do. And I did, sort of. One just needs a little encouragement.

And what about these fucking viruses that tunnel their way under your firewall? A pox on the bastard hackers that cause us such misery! What do they get out of it – power? If they spent as much time on doing something constructive, they'd make millions.

A kid of four knows more about computers and IT than most of the older generation. No wonder there's an ever-widening generation gap, we don't speak the same language any more. Computer repair geniuses talk so quickly I never have the chance to even vaguely understand what the fuck they're talking about. It may as well be in Swahili, which seems to be the language of most call centres these days.

It does worry me that computers now run everything in our lives. As we all know, computers are very temperamental and frustrating in the extreme. Mine suddenly went berserk the other day and I completely lost twenty pages of a document I was working on and I hadn't touched a thing! No matter how much I searched and rang people for assistance, it could not be recovered. It's floating out there somewhere in cyberspace, and I have visions of alien space creatures logging on to it and pissing themselves with laughter at the hysterical stuff I wrote. Jesus never has this problem because 'Jesus saves' I suppose. And how can the cursor just disappear completely? Things move around and change position constantly and it simply refuses to do what I ask of it. It's even worse than my mongrel cat!

I can just picture the Pentagon War Room: 'Er, excuse me, Mr President, we've locked in to a whole heap of nuclear warhead missiles headed this way!'

'What? Well, push the button, man. Activate our Star Wars Anti-Missile Protection Shields immediately!'

'Well, we have a problem, Houston. The computers seem to be having a coffee break or a Nanna Nap. They've gone down. And

I'm not talking Monica Lewinski here. We've got these funny squiggly lines across the screen and the mouse doesn't seem to be working properly and Google's giving me a "This page cannot be displayed" window and another one is saying "You have performed an illegal action and this program will shut down in five minutes". I did manage to get a retaliatory fleet of our missiles away, sir, just before the crash but I think they're headed for Australia.'

And then comes the one word you don't want to hear in a war room: 'Oops.'

Have you ever tried to bring up a Help menu? I need another Help menu to help me understand the Help menu. And the Internet! Okay, it's handy but why do people keep sending me all those stupid jokes and videos about old people? I've got software to protect me from hackers and the reams of spam that offer to lengthen the size of my dick but none to protect me from terrible jokes about Muslims or old people.

Which reminds me, I tried that once. Following Einstein's Theory of Relativity, 'Bigger is Bonzer', I sent off for one of those Penis Enlargement things and they posted me back an elastic strap with a brick attached! Jeez, it hurt when I tried it. And the bloody postage cost me a fortune. It also gave me terrible headaches. Every time a pretty girl passed, the brick bounced up and banged me on the head. Mind you, that was in my more virile days.

I have tried every computer security software I can find, but, try as I may, I can't find one to protect me from comedy pushers who insist on sending me jokes about old age, or chain letters from angels that warn me to pass this on to two hundred friends in ten minutes to get a wonderful surprise or my ass will fall off. Who's got two hundred friends?

After three long months she's discharged. The Neurologist says that they believe she's reached a plateau in rehab and there is nothing more they can do. There's no advice on how to cope or any prognosis; every stroke victim is different, just deal with it.

So, *carefully dressed and made up and wearing her ankle brace, I push her around in her new purple wheelchair while she says farewell to the other patients and thanks the nursing staff and therapists. I wheel her out to the car to begin our new and very different life together. She is so happy to be released from hospital and going home again and we assure each other that somehow we'll learn to cope and, no matter what, our love will carry us through. And so far it has.*

Chapter 7

I read in a book recently that supposedly in the spirit world, souls communicate telepathically and that mankind is slowly redeveloping this ability which was lost in the mists of time when man evolved from spirit into the physical. Maybe it's starting with texting but I hope without the bloody acronyms that now flood our attempts at communicating.

BTW (by the way), GA (Guardian Angel), WTF do I have to do up here? WMH (Where's My Harp)? You want me to R (Reincarnate)? AYBJ (Are You Bloody Joking)? IDLITLT (I Didn't Like It The Last Time).

I recently sat in a restaurant in Paris and watched six Americans at another table frantically web surfing and conversing with each other by text for half an hour without once uttering a single word to each other. I thought they might've been deaf and dumb but eventually they'd obviously decided to leave and texted each other as they all rose as one and chatted about who had paid the bill on line. Apparently they all had. I LMFAO.

And don't talk to me about the ubiquitous smart-arse phones with their thousand-plus apps. Alright, they can be useful sometimes to call an ambulance or the police in case of emergency or when I used to call Marie to see if she was alright alone at home for an hour or so, or for her to call me, usually when I was at the checkout counter, reminding me to get another hundred dollars worth of groceries that weren't on the list and that we'd finish up throwing out. That's fine, but why must we be subjected to other people's unnecessarily loud conversations well within earshot? Like talking about their date last night with lurid sexual connotations, overtones and accompanying giggles, or inane conversations between inane teenagers, or owners talking to their fuckin' pets or, worst of all, boring business conversations. How can people be so rude as to intrude on other people's peaceful inner dialogue or to ignore their companions and send texts or speak to someone else on their bloody phone?

And you're sitting somewhere having a nice cup of coffee, without a cigarette of course, and suddenly you hear these ridiculous ringing tones playing everything from a croaking frog to Beethoven's 7th Symphony and all the other patrons are scrabbling in their handbags and pockets to retrieve their mobiles to settle in for a nice long chat or an inane text conversation. My conversations on receiving a call are inevitably introduced with 'Fuck, fuck, fuck, fuck, fuck!' as I frantically pat my entire body trying to discover in which of my many pockets I had deposited the bloody thing. I then have to separate it from keys, loose change, a nasal spray, eleven different coloured pills and used snotty tissues and try to find the right button to push while the William Tell Overture plays on. Then I remember I have to swipe the bloody screen with my jam donut-coated finger.

I remember accompanying Marie in a disabled toilet and hearing someone outside having a conversation on their mobile saying, 'Yeah, George, I'm outside the disabled toilet in the west side of the shopping mall and if the cripple inside doesn't hurry up I'm gonna wet me pants. She's been in there for hours! What? Well, I like to use the disabled toilet 'cause it's bigger.'

Well, if that doesn't interrupt your pee then nothing will.

Apart from mobile phones, and this is not solely a Withered's gripe, every company you ring now days has that incredibly frustrating answering system that either tells you to hold as your call is very important to them (so answer the fucking call!) or directs you to push buttons from 1 to 100 to get transferred to the next automatic answering service to push more buttons for your selection. By the time I listen carefully to my options I've forgotten who I'm ringing and for what reason. And why the hell do we have customer service call centres in India of all places? The accent is unintelligible and they obviously whisper so as not to disturb the person sitting in the next booth to them and I spend my time screaming, 'Speak louder!' and 'What? What? Listen, I'm a seventy-year-old, English-speaking deaf person and I can't understand a fuckin' word you're saying!'

Have you ever tried to ring Microsoft for technical advice? If you don't speak Hindi, forget it. Read the manual. There you have the choice of at least a dozen foreign languages to confuse you.

She's incontinent for the next year. Every night I wake up to the sound of her night bell every one and a half to two hours, to change her pad or help her to the commode beside the bed. It's driving me crazy and no one seems to be able to help. Eventually I see a program on television with women with the same problem claiming success with the aid of a herbal pill. At this stage I'll try anything. After three months the condition actually improves enormously and she learns to be able to get out of bed by herself and get to the commode without her brace and without my help. One major problem solved, thank God.

Chapter 8

Disabled toilets, or 'Fuckin' Cripple Toilets' as Marie refers to them; now there's a subject for you. I could write a book about disabled toilet experiences. On our first road trip from Brisbane to Melbourne after the stroke, I was a wee bit anxious, so to speak, about toilet facilities for She Who Can't Be Ignored because at that stage if she said, 'I need to stop for the toilet', she meant 'Now!' I carefully studied the road maps trying to find the locations of said toilets and the time it would take to travel in between them. Armed with this information and a map of Australia's Disabled Toilets for Travellers we set off with dubious confidence and a backup plan in case of emergency: a bottle of water, a carton of pads, a large towel, boxes of blotting paper and a bag of Kitty Litter. It was a tense trip. As it turned out, we didn't need the backup plan but you can never be over-confident.

I can remember when she had the incontinence problem, our theme song was that wonderful song of Willie Nelson's, 'On the Commode Again'. There we'd sit, every night, harmonising that classic to keep ourselves awake and stop her from falling off the chair. Another theme song we sang in the car was Ringo Starr's unforgettable 'I Get By With a Little Help From Depends'.

Why is it that most disabled toilets have a bar on one side but not the other? Who designs these contraptions? You can just bet that if your wife needs a right-hand bar it will be on the left side and continue along the back. What's the point of having one running along the back of the pedestal? That is, if you are a woman. She improved her dexterity but she never learned to pee standing up hanging onto the back rail with her one good arm.

In Melbourne, we went to the theatre one night and surprise, surprise, the grab rail was on the right-hand side and as I was helping my wife get off the toilet, I grabbed onto a rail on the left-hand side, which appeared to head up towards the ceiling. The next thing the bar swung down and smashed me on the head. It turned out to be a swivel bar that came down to support you if you were left-hand able. Why hadn't someone thought about that before and why hadn't they warned me before the concussion and bleeding set in?

One day we went to a swish shopping mall and, naturally, had to visit the toilet. It turned out to be an automatic flushing model we hadn't struck before. When you leaned forward, the toilet flushed. Now, my darling wife had been known to go through half a toilet roll in one sitting as she was so particular about her hygiene. Consequently, she eased herself up off the toilet seat quite often to wipe herself, which, at this particular time, proved a little difficult, as every time she leaned forward to wipe, a flood of water gushed out of the system and flooded her nether region. So it became a case of flush, wipe, flush, wipe, flush, wipe. I thought we were going to be stuck in that bloody toilet for a month! Those friggin' 'Mexicans' get all the latest discoveries first.

We found a disabled toilet at Sanctuary Cove on the Gold Coast that has a step up to get into it! Great for wheelchairs! They also have very few ramps from the road to the footpath, which means sometimes you have to go miles to cross the street. And this is supposed to be a millionaires' playground. Maybe they can afford not to be crippled.

Her memory is still remarkably good, thank heavens. But occasionally she gets things wrong which surprises me as her memory was always so reliable. She reminisces a lot about the past, her late parents and childhood, and our thirty-five-year-old son when he was a baby or toddler. Maybe that's not so unusual because we now spend twenty-four hours a day together and there's not a lot else to talk about with such limited activity and uncertain future.

Chapter 9

The day I hit seventy I suddenly knew I was old and once you're over the hill, you certainly pick up speed. It didn't have anything to do with the number of years. After all, I'd been telling people I was eighty since I turned sixty-five and they'd say, 'My God, you look good for your age.' Now I say I'm eighty and they don't turn a hair! No, on my seventieth birthday I suddenly felt old and if it wasn't for the stress, I wouldn't have any visible signs of energy at all. Dry dreams and wet farts weren't so funny anymore. A lot had to do with the fact that I was recovering from my latest hip replacement and after six months I still walked like a drunken drover and got a nagging pain in my gluteus minimus.

Nagging pain always makes me bad-tempered, which is very unusual for me. And doing the housework brings out the worst in me. I'm always dropping things. It's not the dropping that pisses me off; it's the picking up. It's definitely getting harder. It's got to the stage that when I bend down to pick something up or sweep up bits of food or broken bits of china or glass in the dust pan, I take a good look around while I'm down there to see if there's anything else in the vicinity to save me bending down again. I'm thinking of instituting a weekly 'Pick-up Day' when I get down on my hands and knees in the morning and crawl around the entire house for the day picking up things I've dropped. With the amount of litter I seem to accumulate I could wash, dress and feed myself and a family of four while I'm down there.

We have in-home help from one of the charities for five hours a week, and it's marvellous. I come home from grocery shopping and the ironing is done and the house spotless. By that night, after cooking the evening meal and splattering bits of food and other assorted flotsam and jetsam all over the place, it's back to square one.

Vacuum cleaners really suck, except when they don't. White or cream-coloured carpets should be banned or only sold to foreigners who put plastic over their shoes and furniture, or to people who don't go out. I hate it when I'm asked to take my shoes off at the front door. It's so demeaning and infers I'm unclean and sometimes my bare feet are dirtier than the soles of my shoes.

I also hate inanimate things, and that includes some people I know. Inanimate things have a mind of their own. I seem to spend so much time abusing things that don't do what they're supposed to do, or jump out at you when you're not looking. I have had many an argument with inanimate things.

'Yes, that's right, you would do that, wouldn't you, you mongrel bastard!' I scream with my hands on my hips like some affronted transsexual.

Insufferably, they don't say a word. They just ignore you and throw themselves on the floor again, or cut your finger or trip you up, or laugh hysterically as you back into the garage door again because the bastard door decided not to open all the way up. I once ripped off the back door of our van because I forgot to open the garage door fully before I backed out. To be truthful I have had my share of disasters with garage doors but I'm pretty good on the highways as long as there's no traffic. I now have one of those stickers on my car that reads, 'Caution! – Senile Pensioner On Board!' That has made me a desirable target for any hoon on the road.

Chapter 10

My professional life was taken up with being what I call an Iwazza: Iwazza actor, Iwazza director, Iwazza producer, Iwazza writer and finally, when all else failed and I could no longer travel around the countryside working, or the jobs dried up as they inevitably do in our profession, Iwazza teacher. 'Those who can, do. Those who can't …' Still, better to be a has-been than a never-was.

Not being very academically inclined and considering it a waste of limited funds, my parents rightfully decided a University degree was not the wisest course of action for a son who showed a complete lack of any career direction. My father's philosophy that it didn't matter what you did as long as you had a job, propelled me into a series of incredibly boring occupations starting with a position at the *Telegraph* newspaper as a clerk in their library, cutting out and gluing articles and photographs onto sheets of 10x4 and filing them into rows of grey steel filing cabinets. After several bloody and life-threatening paper cuts to my fingers and the result of unintentional glue sniffing, I was transferred to the general office as an office boy and promoted to operating the addressograph machine, printing the names and addresses of subscribers on rolls of paper stickers. This was followed by a brain numbing clerical job for the Brisbane City Council Electricity Department of Inspections, and an equally soul-destroying career as a counter salesman for the esteemed Rothwell's Gentlemen's Outfitters, where I rose to the dizzying heights of Manager of the gentlemen's jocks-and-socks underwear department in which I steadfastly refused to carry out personal fittings.

This was interrupted by three months of compulsory National Service in the Army where I excelled at marksmanship, precision marching, drill, and screaming obscenities while I bayoneted stuffed dummies. However, strangely, this did not encourage me to consider a career in the armed forces as I didn't relish the thought of being screamed at, bayoneted, garrotted, shot at or blown up.

I returned to civilian life and for some strange reason (I think it was money) accepted a job as an industrial chemical salesman, which was weird as industrial chemistry had never been a subject which fascinated me or even vaguely interested me. Eventually, by mutual consent and to the relief of both parties, we parted company.

By now I had at last discovered my true vocation – the joy of acting – 'The Thetah' and the dizzy glamour of showbiz. My introduction to this exciting milieu was instigated by a casual meeting with a friend, Barry Creighton, who was later to achieve stardom in Australian television in the hugely successful *Mavis Bramston Show*, who invited me to attend a Club Night at the prestigious Brisbane Arts Theatre. A whole new world opened up to me and I soon found myself completely involved in the craft of acting. I had at last found my niche in life.

I attended private speech and drama classes with the theatre company's founder, Jean Trundle, and soon found myself being cast in their productions. I received excellent reviews for my performances which I unreservedly considered raves, and after a few years extended my abilities to include directing. By this time I had met the love of my life and after nine months of 'courting' we were married and blissfully happy.

Television came knocking when Channel 7 asked me to join George Wallace Jr's top-rating *Theatre Royal* and *Club 7* comedy company where I turned fully professional and honed my skills in television comedy, singing and dancing in this fairly recently developed industry.

After three years and with the sad discovery that, medically, it was unlikely that we would ever become parents, we decided to move to Melbourne and pursue our careers in the emerging but uncertain world of Australian Stage and Television. In spite of the uncertainty in this fledgling industry we naively believed that talent would out and we would survive. It wasn't easy but somehow we did.

In the Golden Age of the fifties and sixties, actors had to speak proper. Years were spent developing our breathing, voices, speech and acting technique and there's no way you'd get a job if you had a discernible Australian accent, or your diction or projection were inadequate. Nowadays if you speak well you're frowned upon, and seen as being quaint, old-fashioned, a bit of a wanker and irrelevant to the industry. Surprisingly, one of the most common whinges I hear from other Withereds is the decline in the use of the English language. They complain about pronunciation, clarity, the lack of correct spelling and grammar and the obligatory overuse of the four-letter word. Well, fuck me!

My theory as to speech – although it is constantly changing and growing to fulfil the current needs of communication – is the ability to allow the listener to hear and understand you clearly and in that way, avoid a misunderstanding that could lead to insult, violence or, in extreme cases, world war. Politicians and generals, not speaking the same language as other politicians and generals of the country they are attempting to subjugate, democratise and manipulate, who are working through interpreters, must be the cause of a lot of international strife.

Today, with the advances in microphones and audio equipment, the fashion is to mumble and whisper on camera for the sake of 'realism', and with a penchant for accents, to make it even more realistic. That's all very well if you come from the same English county as the actor but if you live in an English-speaking country across the other side of the world and your hearing isn't exactly one hundred percent, you're in deep shit.

And why have they increased the volume of atmospheric background noise and the music soundtrack? I know television and film are 'visual' media but if you aren't supposed to hear or understand the dialogue, why bother with the bloody script? In the latter part of my career I sometimes had to be jabbed with a long stick when it was my turn to speak as I couldn't hear the bloody cue.

In America, of course, as Professor Higgins in *Pygmalion* says, 'They haven't spoken English for years', so one can expect little else. At one stage in America, would you believe, Australian films were classified as foreign films! But I believe sub-titles should be compulsory for all television and film, then we'd really see how bad the scripts are.

A successful actor friend of mine – and you can count those on one hand, both a successful actor, or a friend – one who is of the same vintage as I, puts a lot of the problem down to what he calls the Show Off Your Beautiful Teeth Syndrome but I think it's because their Botoxed lips never once have the chance to meet over those perfect, white, dentally engineered teeth so the words that contain any consonant that requires the lips to actually touch are completely unintelligible. Lazy tongues are another problem and I find with my students, the only time young people exercise their tongues is when they're French kissing or practising cunnilingus.

Anyway, being a professional actor is a really silly occupation. By nature, it turns you into a self-centred, egotistical, psychological misfit, desperately selling yourself to survive. We kid ourselves that we're being 'creative' when we're frantically trying to get ourselves noticed and saying to the world, 'Look at me, I exist!' To make a buck we have to accept pretty well anything that's offered to us: theatre, television roles, film and even commercials. I've done some very embarrassing things in my career and all for the buck and the chance to be noticed by producers and directors and to eat and keep a roof over our heads. Various directors can be as psychologically unstable and desperate as we are. The mothers of some young, would-be-actor children are positively embarrassing, living their dreams through their offspring. These pathetic, misguided mums have damaged many a young kid's life by trying to push them into the soul-destroying celebrity spotlight. But what really pisses me off is I was never once inveigled, or even invited, onto a 'casting couch'!

I have asked many young trainee actor children I have been forced to teach, why they want to be actors, and they inevitably reply, 'I don't know, I just want to be famous and on television.' For the thousands of actors trying to make a living in the industry and with periods of 'resting', only a handful will ever make it to international stardom but there are a lot of talented people out there who are willing to take the chance of finding steady work not for the stardom but for a love of acting. If you're hooked you really have little choice. Their chances of making a living from it are less than one hundred to one and can lead to much heartache and disappointment. It's really sad to be so insecure. For God's sake, if people want to act for the love of it, do it in a non-professional company where you can have fun! It can build character and help develop your personality.

But as Noel Coward said, 'Don't put your daughter on the stage, Mrs Worthington', unless you have a family trust. The dream is sometimes more attractive than the achievement.

I have to learn to be careful about the awful sadness that envelops me at every unguarded moment; my wife unsteadily trying to make me a cup of tea, struggling out of her chair and making her way to the toilet and back, getting in and out of the car, trying to dress or undress herself without help, or simply moving from one spot to another. Old photographs that used to bring back happy memories now bring a tear. Memories are dangerous things; not the sad ones, the happy ones. I wonder if that is why a lot of old people lose their memory? Maybe they don't want to remember. Maybe it hurts too much to know that it's all gone. Enough!

Chapter 11

I know The Media is a favourite hobbyhorse for nearly all us Withereds, the unbelievably stupid rubbish that surrounds the few intelligent shows that slip through. Sometimes I think it's a shame to interrupt the flow of commercials to slot in a few minutes of the show you're trying to watch. It really riles me when the presenter of the news or current affair programs says, 'We wish to advise viewers that the next report contains images and material that may offend some viewers.' Well, don't fuckin' show it!

Chat show hosts drive me insane with their over-bright, sparkling American smiles and feverish energy begging us to love them. I'm appalled when a journalist asks inane and intrusive questions of an emotional parent or loved one, after a death or fatal road accident, with the obvious intention of getting a few tears of suffering on camera. And the guest interviewees on 'talk shows' are even worse. How can people go on camera in front of millions of viewers and unashamedly weep buckets of tears and go on and on about their boring and embarrassing personal problems. Who gives a shit? Obviously, according to the so-called 'independent' ratings, millions of people do. Is it because we feel smug seeing other people suffering and worse off than we are? Is that why hospital or doctor TV series are so incredibly popular? I thought they put you to sleep during an operation so you don't have to watch. But if it's someone else being cut up, I suppose that's 'entertainment'.

I actually saw a segment the other night on one of those incredibly vapid commercial current affair shows where they demonstrated how to hang out your washing! I mean, really! How much intelligence does it take to stick a clothes peg on your undies? If it hurts your brain too much to work it out, throw it all in the dryer! Actually, I must admit, my mother-in-law used to sneak around spying on other people's washing, muttering under her breath, 'Huh, look at the way he's hung that towel right next to that shirt, which, incidentally, he's hung upside down, and look how many pegs he's used! He's obviously a bachelor, but I don't think he's a homosexual, because homosexual men are so tidy and precise. Yes, you can always pick a gay man's washing.'

Is it true that eighty percent of Oprah's viewers got all their information on world events from a fat again, thin again, fat again, thin again, charismatic talk show lady host who held more influence over the population than the President of the United States? Mind you, that was understandable when George Bush was President. It's a wonder they didn't vote for Oprah as President but I doubt the viewers would get off their fat asses to vote because they were too lazy or too comfortable sitting down and watching her on TV and chomping on munchies and flinging back Coke.

Another thing that really trounces my time zones is 'Television Tardiness'. If they advertise a program as starting at eight-thirty, is it too outrageously impatient of me to expect it at eight-thirty and not eight-fifty? All the channels do it. Because one channel is running late, I have to miss the end of one program to catch the start of the next program on another channel, only to find out they're also running late and I either have to go to the toilet, or channel swap between the two, or sit through and watch the last ten or fifteen minutes of a show I didn't want to see in the first place.

When I was directing television dramas it was essential we brought the show in at an exact time to the minute as our show was not to run overtime on pain of death or worse, retrenchment. What happened to that rule? Are the channels creeping in extra commercial time? That would be against the Australian Broadcasting rules, wouldn't it? Or are they deliberately doing it to hold viewers onto the same channel for their next piece of shit? Sneaky, manipulative bastards!

And don't start me on 'reality' television. Reality is not all that interesting or attractive in the first place. All reality TV programs have to be heavily edited and constructed to make them appear even slightly interesting and 'real', and even then they fail to grab me by the short and curlies. Do we really need to see shots of people being killed, tortured or bleeding, or being bashed senseless, in graphic colour? I don't think so. It desensitises our minds and all these horrific images have now become acceptable. No one will ever convince me that they don't affect the minds of children or viewers who are just a little left of centre in the brain department. Graphic television dramas are also unreal because the viewer doesn't have the actual lighting, atmosphere or smells that accompany the hospital, accident or war zones, which, in real life, would surely make us chuck up, pass out or run screaming from the scene.

Why are hospital dramas so popular? What is so attractive about watching sick people suffering, or operations with lots of blood? I never found it attractive when visiting sick loved ones, or having an operation myself. I do remember when I was about to have my vasectomy saying to the surgeon, just before I went under, 'Now, whatever happens, don't be nervous. I don't want your hand shaking while you're snipping away at my balls.' That got a laugh.

What is this 'stubble on the face' syndrome that has become so popular with television presenters, film actors and models? Why is it fashionable to look like you've just got out of bed and haven't had time to shave, wash your face and comb your hair? And that's just the women. What about self-respect, and making yourself look as clean and presentable as possible with what you've got to work with, for the people who have got to look at you? Don't force your rumpled grubbiness on us. If I go for one day without shaving, She Who Can't Be Ignored soon lets me know her views in no uncertain terms.

'What about Russell Crowe and Hugh Jackman and all those other butch actors you see on the screen?' I retort, defensively. 'I'm trying to look more rugged and masculine and with it.'

'Well,' she says, 'firstly, I don't have to kiss them goodnight and get stubble rash, and secondly, their stubble is black and they don't look like some trainee, underfed Santa Claus, and thirdly you don't look *with it*, you look *withered*.'

Oh well, there goes the chic and out with the Schick.

I remember when Don Johnson from *Miami Vice* started the fashion of not wearing socks, my runners ended up smelling like a polar bear had crapped in them.

And let's not get on to commercials. Don't insult my intelligence, please. Just tell me what it is, where I can get it, and how much. I'm so sick of everybody trying to sell me something in living, breathing colour, with impossibly beautiful twenty-year-old models advertising age-defying creams and lotions. Don't bother! If I really need, and can't live without, yet another new and improved razor that will make me as sexy as the handsome, young buff in the advertisement, that not only cuts me with three blades, but can positively shred me to pieces with four, while vibrating and playing beautiful music as the blood trickles down the drain, I'll fuckin' buy one!

I hate the constantly repeated commercials about Prostate Clinics and Pee Pads and Sanitary Napkins. There was a poor guy on a prostate clinic ad, leaking like a dripping tap, looking miserable; which was not at all funny. But on the bright side, think of the night-time exercise he's gets: up and down out of bed and running to the toilet, with his old wife hanging over his shoulder. I'd never let my wife hang over my shoulder while I was peeing.

And don't scream at me in million-decibel, hi-fi, fake Australian or American accents, not to miss this, never to be repeated again and this week only, incredible, tacky rug bargain, at seventy percent off. I'll wait until the fabulous sixties hessian model I have wears out. I don't care if you're having a constant 'bargain sale' at eighty percent off, just don't scream at me! And I'm certainly not going to buy a squillion-dollar car, high-fashion threads and accessories, or a three-hundred-centimetre television set with matching DVD, and theatre surround sound, home entertainment system, that will only work until the day the guarantee runs out. No sir; not until they lift the pension rate and feed the starving millions in Africa.

You'll notice that most advertising, except for the Prostate Clinic, Pee Protection Pads and the like, is aimed at the under fifties. That's because us oldies are far too smart to be sucked in by such blatant hype and lies, except the ones about creams that make you look younger. No, all commercials should be funny and star meerkats or other funny animals. Give us a laugh while you're trying to screw us.

I have to admit I'm a TV remote control junkie and it drives She Who Can't Be Ignored crazy. I was happily clicking away the other night trying to avoid the dreaded commercials, when suddenly I was confronted with a program explaining the virtues of vibrators! Now television, at its rare best, can be educational, or so we are told, and I have to admit my education in vibrators has been sadly neglected, so I allowed myself to be sucked in, so to speak. Despite the fact that it was a trifle embarrassing to watch with my wife sitting a few feet away, I persisted, and allowed the blood to pump into my face, the only significant area it does tend to pump into these days. Not only were we confronted with vibrators of every shape, size and colour, but a running commentary from designers, manufacturers and users! I was totally mesmerised. I never knew the vibrator industry was so high-tech.

I believe the company's name was 'TWAT', an acronym for The Women's Aerodynamic Tingler.

Her left side is so sensitive the slightest touch hurts her. People constantly pat her or put their arm around her shoulder and she winces. Lying in bed I touch her left elbow and say, 'Can you feel where I'm touching?' And she'll say 'My wrist?' or 'My shoulder?' She has no idea if she can't actually see where you're touching. If she tries to move her left arm her left leg shoots out. To move her left foot she has to look down at it because she doesn't know where it is. A stand-up or lying-down one-arm cuddle is very awkward and uncomfortable for her. She was always such a warm, 'touching' person who enjoyed our love making. It's so hard to relate to this and my memory keeps returning to happier days.

The Two of Us and *Perryman on Parade* with Jill Perryman. A delight to work with

Clowning it up with Jill Perryman on ABC's *Perryman on Parade*

Premiere of *Libido*. Pregnant on the red carpet

A few weeks later Benjamin Daniel premieres

The Theatre needed me

Tied up by Alfred Sandor in an episode of *Ryan*

With Nancy Cato, Marie Redshaw and Joe James in *Say Who You Are*

Marie as the cop's wife in *Matlock Police*

My first experience in Theatre Restaurant. Why?

Chapter Two by Neil Simon

The hilarious Jan Russ at the Stage Door Dinner Theatre

With Barb Ramsay, Will Deumer and Jan Russ
at the Stage Door Dinner Theatre

Kiss Me Goodnight Sergeant Major
with Barb Ramsay, Will Deumer and Berrie Cameron Allen

Chapter 12

We met at a cast party at the Brisbane Arts Theatre on Petrie Terrace, in 1958. I was new to the group and a little uneasy about attending my first sophisticated social cocktail party, which were so popular then and now replaced by drunken booze-ups and violent binge drinking. I walked in with a friend and nervously smiled at a few unfamiliar faces that turned to check out this new, sexy talent on the scene. We grabbed a couple of glasses of cheap wine and began circulating. I chatted with a few friendly young folk about the same age as myself while letting my eyes wander around the room, doing my own secretive checking of the available 'talent'. And there she was: standing tall in her six-inch heels, blonde hair pulled back in a French roll to camouflage her unruly curls, slender with a figure to die for and beautifully dressed in a slim-fitting turquoise sheath dress with just enough cleavage showing to capture your attention. And she was looking straight at me! And smiling! Her eyes were a fascinating flecked blue-green that changed colour with the shade of dress she wore.

As I casually sauntered over towards her, pretending indifference, as one does in the mating game, she turned to her female friend and continued her whispered conversation whilst turning her back to me. I noticed the neckline on the back of her dress was cut low revealing her seductive, pale shoulders and back. An accidental gesture on her part, I'm sure.

I found out many years later that she'd whispered to her friend after she saw me and I was doing my macho but sophisticated glide towards her, 'Wow, I'm gonna have that one.' And she eventually did. After a whirlwind courtship, we were engaged on April Fool's Day of 1960, which I never let her forget, and we were married on December 17th. The wedding ceremony was held in the beautiful, but as then unfinished, Gothic St John's Cathedral and a photograph in the Brisbane Courier Mail the following day was headlined, 'Shakespearean Sweethearts Wed'. I had never seen a more beautiful bride.

We continued working in the Arts Theatre and learning our trade by experience and from totally committed teachers, fellow actors and directors who believed only the highest standard was acceptable. It was a rare and exciting apprenticeship and Marie distinguished herself in many leading and diverse roles ranging from Eliza Dolittle in George Bernard Shaw's *Pygmalion*; Sally Bowles in Christopher Isherwood's *I am a Camera (Cabaret)*, to many modern and Shakespearian roles. Her colouring, bearing and personality gave her a wonderful glow on stage and the effect was mesmerising to an inexperienced actor and husband such as myself.

But I learned quickly and within a few busy years had been invited to join the cast of BTQ Channel 7's top-rating, live-to-air variety show *Theatre Royal*. I also made regular appearances in *Club 7*, another live-to-air variety show. Channel 7 was like a little Hollywood in those days, with famous variety performers of the time and gorgeous chorus girls strutting their stuff around the studio and canteen. So, two television shows a week kept me pretty busy doing comedy sketches, singing and dancing, so I gave up my boring day job as an industrial chemical salesman and became a full-time professional.

The fire had been lit and would not be extinguished. We had just built our first home in Indooroopilly when we discovered that it was medically doubtful that we would ever be able to have a family of our own so we decided to take the plunge and do what we really loved. We rented out the house and moved to Melbourne in January 1968 to gain further experience before planning to take off to London, which was the ultimate destination in the seventies for stage actors not recognised for their work in their home country.

I was lucky and in the right place at the right time and worked fairly constantly for the first few years, gaining acceptance and reputation. I auditioned for the St Martin's Theatre Company and was soon offered a part in the British World War One classic, *Oh, What a Lovely War*. The show was sold to J.C. Williamson's and moved to Sydney with a return season in Melbourne and we had our first taste of being on tour with a show, which was marvellous. When Marie nervously auditioned for St Martin's, she announced to the director she would be performing a dramatic speech from the classic *Saint Joan*, took a deep breath, opened her mouth and out came a comedy monologue with a lisp from a review she had performed a couple of years before in Brisbane. She didn't pass the audition process.

She found office work for which she was very well equipped and worked as a highly responsible Girl Friday/bookkeeper for an employment agency and later as a valued administrator for a War Widows' Guild Hostel and Nursing Home for aged war widows to help support us while insisting I continue with my acting career. Previous to this she took the occasional television acting job and won a regular role as the Sergeant's wife in Crawford's *Matlock Police* series. As was usual in that period, acting work for men was slightly more abundant than for women.

Five years later, we were astounded and delighted to learn Marie had fallen pregnant. She intentionally retired from her acting career in favour of my continuing as she believed marriage and family, which are a bit dodgy in the industry, were more important to her than her personal ambition. And, of course, it was easier to keep an eye on me and keep me in line if we weren't separated for long stretches of time. She was no fool. During the seventies she had suffered a couple of painful miscarriages, one of which occurred while I was away from home, tutoring at a young actors' workshop at Geelong Grammar. She didn't notify me at the time because she didn't want to interrupt my work and I didn't find out until I returned home to discover her in terrible pain, being cared for by a friend.

Moving overseas and starting over again was no longer an option and we continued to live in Melbourne, comfortably surviving as a loving family.

During this time and BB – before Ben – my agent signed me to a contract for the Killara Community Theatre Company in Sydney so we moved up there for a couple of years and rented a flat in Cameray. Marie went off the next day to hunt for an office job and, as usual, was quite successful and asked to start at the beginning of the next week. I immediately went into rehearsals for an English farce, the name of which escapes me, *Dial M for Murder*, in which

I played the dastardly husband, and *Hamlet*, in which I played Banquo's ghost. Not actually a leading role, but it did keep me offstage a lot and away from the horrendous high school student audiences who were forced to study this Shakespearian classic. Playing Shakespeare to a predominantly high school student audience was an actor's nightmare in those days. I wonder if it's changed.

Feeling a bit financially flush, we went berserk and bought a second-hand Austin Cambridge from one of the questionable car dealers in Western Sydney and headed back to visit family and friends in Brisbane. Now I admit my mechanical knowledge is a bit limited to, is it comfortable, a nice colour, has it got brakes and four wheels, kicking the tyres and checking the outside for any rust. We had to call roadside assistance three times on the trip north, only to be towed to the nearest country garage where every mechanic or proprietor would look under the hood (which I thought was very knowledgeable) and peer at the engine and say, 'Hm, big motor. She needs oil and new spark plugs.' It cost us more in oil and spark plugs than it did in petrol but we finally arrived in Brisbane where we were told it needed a new head gasket, more spark plugs and several hundred dollars' worth of repairs. Not the cheapest excursion. We returned to Sydney and traded the monster in on a much more reliable Volkswagen Beetle. It was comfortable, nice colour and upholstery, no exterior rust and had four wheels. Perfect.

I was then asked to audition for Harry M Miller's production of *Boys in the Band*. It was a cattle call audition which meant you sat around for hours with a hundred other hopefuls eyeing off the competition and waiting to be called. The play was about a homosexual birthday party and very controversial at that time. Written by Mart Crowley, it was hilariously funny but also tender and moving. I was fortunate to be cast as the lead character, Michael, who remains on stage for the entire performance and runs the gamut of emotions from brittle comedy through to a nervous collapse toward the end.

It was reported to me that John Krummel, who played the part and was magnificent in the original production a couple of years earlier, was forced to exit the stage during one performance and relieve himself in the rather restricted wing space into one of the many wine bottles used in the production without pausing in the delivery of his lines. He then returned onto the stage, mid speech, carrying the steaming bottle of 'wine' and offered it around his guests. Understandably they all declined. Fortunately, I never had to resort to pissing in a prop but it came close sometimes.

We played to packed houses and excellent reviews touring the east coast of Australia for several months, playing in the large theatres of Newcastle, Brisbane, Sydney and Melbourne. It was a great thrill to return to my home city of Brisbane playing the lead in such a controversial and long-awaited show and the audiences were amazing. I received a memorable standing ovation on my first entrance but I think that was mostly due to the fact that the play had eventually arrived in Queensland. It was the first time Brisbane audiences were allowed to hear the infamous four letter words and they went crazy. One of the critics on opening night noted that the male audience looked far prettier than the females.

In other states we would inevitably be visited by the Vice Squad who would then instruct us as to the words that were not acceptable in their city. In Newcastle, one of the lines that had to be cut was the notorious, 'Who do you have to fuck to get a drink around here?' The detective suggested it be changed to, 'Who do you have to SUCK around here to get a drink?'. Yeah, much more tasteful.

In Melbourne I couldn't say, 'You look like shit but I'm impressed.' But I could say, 'You look like BULLSHIT but I'm impressed.' (?) Not the same rhythm at all.

But in Brisbane we could let it all hang out and I think the theatre got four complaints. How times have changed. Nowadays you hear fuck seemingly every second word on stage, television and film. I suppose you could say the casts of both *Boys in the Band* companies, for better or worse, helped to abolish restrictive censorship and change what is now accepted on Australian stage, film and television.

The week after we returned to Sydney I was asked to fly to Melbourne for a guest role in the Crawford's police series, *Division 4*. The guest role was a suspiciously gay master criminal, who wore beautiful suits and carried a large sword for some strange reason. The next two roles I was offered on television were also both gay characters as a result of my success in *Boys in the Band* and I then drew the line and made it known that I didn't want to be typecast and turned down the part of the gay character in *The Box*, which eventually went to Paul Karo who received a silver Logie for the role. I was then offered a role in a new Australian musical, *Caroline*, and a series of plays in Melbourne so we decided we may as well move back to that beautiful city as our home base.

I was so thrilled to be cast in *The Two of Us*, a two-handed comedy, co-starring with the beautiful and wonderfully talented star of Australian musical comedy, Jill Perryman, in her first straight role and which played to packed houses. This was followed with a co-starring role with Nancye Hayes and Rod Muliner in Neil Simon's *Star Spangled Girl*, the lead in *The Winslow Boy* and another season of ABC's *Bellbird* to keep me in work and my family supplied with luxuries like food, shelter and clothing. I continued to make many regular guest appearances in the Crawford stable of television shows and other ABC productions.

After submitting a script to Reg Grundy Productions, I was contracted as a scriptwriter for two years for the long-running *Prisoner* series, whilst appearing on camera as the semi-regular psychiatrist character, Dr Weissmann, and believe me, with a cast the majority of which were women who fancied themselves as 'International Stars', a psychiatrist was certainly essential. I also appeared in a few best-forgotten films. one of which, *Libido,* required me to strip naked for a shower scene and appear in a very tasteless orgy scene to the delight of the female crew members and a couple of the guys. But it did get me a trip to the Tehran Film Festival representing the Australian entry. That was during the time when the Shah was still in power and the political intrigue was stirring. It was exciting and I got to meet a few of my international film idols at the festival. I was loath to go as our son, Benjamin, was only a few months old at the time and I didn't want to leave Marie alone with him to look after but she insisted that I attend.

I signed a contract with Crawford Productions, the largest independent television production company in the country at that time, and directed the top-rating *Division 4*, starring a friend from Queensland, Gerard Kennedy, and *The Box*, a controversial program in opposition to the Sydney production of the equally controversial *Number 96*, for Channel 10. I was retrenched when Crawford's lost several of their shows after a dispute over more Australian content than overseas content for which we fought so hard. Ah well, that's showbiz. Feeling disgruntled with the industry, I accepted a very lucrative offer to appear in a highly successful, bawdy Theatre Restaurant that shall remain nameless, which further damaged my love of the traditional theatre, and determined me to aim for more personal satisfaction and creative expression.

To this end, with a business partner and actor friend, Barbara Ramsay, who had trained at the prestigious American Julliard Academy and whom I had worked with previously in television and in the aforesaid highly popular Theatre Restaurant, mortgaged our homes to the hilt and opened, owned and operated the Stage Door Dinner Theatre in the late seventies and early eighties. I continued to act and write for television while Marie held down a permanent administrative position for a War Widows' Guild Aged Care facility. We leased an old printing factory in South Melbourne, gutted the interior and set to work on what turned out to be a very ambitious (some might say crazy) and exhausting enterprise. Having no previous experience in catering or running a restaurant, it was a daunting task renovating, hiring a chef and staff, while writing, producing and appearing in shows and overseeing the overall management of the project. We presented both musicals and plays such as Neil Simon's *Chapter Two* and many musical revues which we wrote and performed in ourselves, with dinner provided for the audience in the intervals. It gave me the opportunity to work with such talented people as the wonderfully funny Jan Russ, Annie Phelan, Berrie Cameron Allen, Paul Karo, the late Marie Redshaw and a dear and talented friend, Will Deumer.

We opened with *Kiss Me Goodnight Sergeant Major*, a nostalgic musical revue Barb and I wrote, based on the WW2 period, and which was later bought by the South Australian Arts Council for an Adelaide production. Marie made an enormous contribution in menu control, costume design and sewing while holding down a full-time job and overseeing our son's upbringing. She would just get in and do anything that needed doing with a firm hand and without serious complaint. Her energy and commitment were staggering.

The constant pressure eventually took its toll and finally becoming disenchanted with acting and the entertainment industry, we sold our share of the business in 1985. I continued writing and performing in guest roles and eventually accepted a position as manager of the hugely successful Dracula's Cabaret Restaurant in Melbourne, and introduced the concept of having comedy/horror waiters and waitresses. I christened myself 'Rigor Mortis'. I later transferred to the Gold Coast as the manager of their new venue in Surfers Paradise. Like it or not the entertainment industry was all that I knew.

At last, with the realisation that 'those who can, do, and those who can't, teach', I was offered speech and acting tutorial work for the Australian Film and Television Academy and Warner Bros Movie World theme park.

Life took a drastic change when Marie suffered the stroke and I became her full-time carer. I retired from the acting profession and the entertainment industry to concentrate on looking after Marie, writing, and eventually becoming a successful novelist. Still waiting on that one.

I admit, at times, I had to accept some pretty awful and sometimes demeaning work to survive in the industry but survive we did. I would like it to go on record that in the thirty-five years of my career, I was not once ever invited or coerced onto the 'casting couch'. How insulting is that?!

There's good and bad in any career and you just have to suck it up and push on and get your priorities right. My priorities have always been for the welfare of my wife and son so there was no dispute in my mind.

During that time we had our troubles and disagreements as any young couple would, but it was largely Marie's support and determination that made our marriage work without ever losing her self-respect or her unconditional love and respect for me.

Chapter 13

Now sex used to be one of my favourite subjects, and although not an actual pastime anymore, I remember it as more of a private thing. My little tadpoles may now have turned into toads and I barely remember my first experience. I know I was alone at the time reading some educational literature; I think it was a Playboy magazine, the epitome of sexual education at that time. But we didn't talk about it much then, and we certainly didn't see it on film or television. That would've spoiled the guilt thing. Now it's all taken for granted and displayed in the most lurid detail. I can remember the only sex advice I got from mother was 'only do it with people you love.' By God, I fell in love with a lot of ugly women.

I remember trying to have a sex education talk with my then pubescent son. I thought I was doing pretty well until suddenly he interrupted me with 'It's okay, Dad, I know all about that stuff.' Really? I thought. Now I know where to go when I need some advice.

And then there was a lovely-looking girl I went out with for a while in my rampant youth. But every time I kissed her goodnight, she farted! I must've been pushing the wrong button. The relationship didn't last. It played hell with my sinus.

We all knew that masturbation sent you blind, and there was a good chance your hand would drop off. I remember feeling so sorry for an old blind guy with one arm, tapping his white cane down the street near the local Catholic High School, and the kids yelling out to him, 'Dirty bugger!'

It's hard to keep up with the mysterious ailments she develops. She has an itching problem and none of the 'experts' seem to be able to offer a solution. The closest I can get is that it's an allergy. But an allergy to what, we can't find out. With only one working hand it's impossible for her to reach most of the trouble spots and I'm constantly being asked to scratch them for her. How annoying it must be for her. Something else I'd never thought of before; not to be able to scratch an itchy spot must drive her crazy.

Call me old fashioned but I really have difficulty coping with copulation on film or television; men with women, men with men, women with women. I even have trouble with animals rooting. Do we really need to see everything? I think not. What happened to the old days when the actors would get to a certain point in their lovemaking, always with closed mouth kissing I might add, and there would be a discreet fade to black, or a slow pan to the window and a shot of the tempestuous storm raging outside with waves crashing on the shore, or an explosion of fireworks, , or a rocket being launched, and the rest would be left up to our own imagination, or acceptable level of perversion. You never would've seen Bette Davis with her gear off simulating an orgasm with a naked, Richard Widmark, which was definitely a good thing.

It's okay when you're doing it yourself in privacy but squirming around on top of each other in every conceivable angle, position and location, with all the accompanying heavy breathing, groping, groaning, moaning, panting and squishing, being watched by an entire world of voyeurs, is a little disconcerting. What is the difference between reality, art and pornography, by the way? Sometimes I long for that dirty word 'censorship'. There are a lot of mentally sick people out there and it's probably better that the rest of us do without a bit of over-explicit sex to prevent over-exciting the sickos.

I suppose watching David Attenborough, who seems to have a definite penchant for copulating animals, birds, fish, reptiles and even insects, on his wildlife programs, probably could be construed as 'educational' or even titillating if you happen to be into bestial practices, but watching our own species copulate is somewhat embarrassing. They always seem to last much longer than I do and reach even bigger climaxes. I can do without the comparison, thank you.

When you sit having a cup of coffee – without a cigarette of course – on the sidewalk or in a shopping mall, watching life's passing parade, and contemplating its myriad depressing facets, you realise there are very few really attractive people in the world, and the thought of these plain, obese or anorexic, spotty, scruffy and downright ugly-looking individuals that invade my vision, actually copulating, breeding and producing WLKs (Weird Looking Kids) is horrifying. Yet I'm assured in all the sex literature in graphic magazines that I read in the doctor's waiting room, that everybody, or at least most of us who can still remember, are driven by sex. So most of these strange-looking people obviously find someone to do it with, it seems. Maybe I should frequent a higher class of shopping centre. I've started referring to our shopping mall as 'Ugly City'.

There's so little privacy available to us now but there's always somewhere secluded to vent your lust, like in the back row of a half-empty cinema while you're watching an 'M' or 'R' rated film or nodding off in *Les Mis*. Or what about in your own home with the doors firmly shut, the curtains drawn and the sound system up to its maximum volume? And those weird people who take selfies or video themselves having sex and have the audacity to post them online should learn how to play Scrabble or Dominos, not Sexual Snakes and Ladders and Tantric Twister.

Here's a thought: with all the computerised automated slot machines we have today, why hasn't someone come up with a computerised, automated, shagging slot machine? I'm sure it would make a million. It would do away with brothels and allow the girls to go into "nice" careers like modelling or computer programming. I'm sure it would seriously dent the number of rapes in the community, and I know some of the wives would definitely welcome it.

Just think about it: you could have themed cubicles containing lots of warm, vibrating, sensual plastic images, flattering lighting, soft music and a plasma screen showing hi-tech porno movies.

'Excuse me, love, while you're at Woolies doing the grocery shopping, I might just pop in to the Heaven's Delight slot machine arcade and have a quickie. You got change of twenty in two-dollar coins?'

With the approach of old age the most difficult thing to contemplate is the future and what it might hold. My imagination runs wild with scenes of horror that may befall us: Nursing Homes, senility or Alzheimer's, debilitating illnesses, becoming too frail to look after Marie. Most carers must have the same fears.

This is a futile and dangerous exercise and I must avoid it as much as possible. But there are unguarded times when the black chasm of despair envelopes my mind and the gates of dreaded possibilities are thrown open. I must train myself not to project the future and take one day, or even one moment, at a time.

Chapter 14

Speaking of music, I haven't understood a lyric since the Beatles came to power. I thought at first it was just the demise of my hearing, but I can understand every word on the ABC news. I have no trouble hearing the lyrics on the Community Radio Station for Oldies, with their wonderful 50s and 60s classics by Dean Martin and Nat King Cole and the like, and those wonderful titles and lyrics, like Herman's Hermits' 'Mrs Brown You've Got a Lovely Walker', or the fabulous Bobby Darrin's 'Splish Splash, I Was Takin' a Slash', or 'Once, Twice, Three Times to the Bathroom', by the Commodes. What's the point of having lyrics if you can't understand them or relate to them?

While we're on the Arts, and seeing I am, as yet, an unrecognised talent of the acrylic and oil palette, I believe this gives me the right to have my say on the subject. I have a very definite opinion on Art; if I like it, it's good, if I don't, it's bad.

All the furore about Bill Henshaw photographing a naked thirteen-year-old girl frankly astounded me. There is no doubt his work is incredibly beautiful, and if he had painted her in oils, nobody would have said a thing. Most of the Old Masters painted naked young girls and nobody jumped up and down asking how old the model was. But if you photograph her, that's an entirely different matter it seems.

Now I wouldn't think there'd be a lot of dirty old men wandering around art galleries who are interested in child pornography. But there again I may be wrong. I've seen a lot of weird-looking types hanging around galleries but I always put it down to their being 'Arty'. But from recent reports on child pornography it would appear that the range of would-be child molesters stretches from bishops to blue-collar workers and beyond so you never know where they'll turn up.

That also makes me realise that this perverted urge has always been with mankind. It's only with the advent of the terrible television and mass media that we are now constantly being bombarded with it. Perhaps Bill Henshaw was a little too liberal in his artistic endeavours for today's world but remember Reuben was over fifty years old when he bedded and married a fifteen year old and no one was outraged when he constantly painted her in the nude. Forget the zoom lens, Bill, and pick up a number four sable brush and splosh the image on a canvas, or better still, paint your old Kodak box camera in different colours and add a few bits of wire netting and a feather. Now, that's art!

Another art I'm particularly interested in is cooking, particularly cooking with wine. I have even been known to throw in the odd bit of food occasionally. I'm really learning to hate Nutritionists. They've ruined some of my best recipes. It's such yet another con. If you're obese, then don't eat so much! Everywhere you look there's another expert or Guru on food and nutrition, telling us why we should or should not eat or drink this or that. It's actually a very inexpert science at this time, as they don't know exactly how the various molecular structures react with each other in natural food. Isolate one protein and it may upset the balance without another.

They identified and extracted carotene from carrots and lauded it as being a super healthy ingredient, but now they find it doesn't work without the rest of the carrot structure. After years of telling us that a glass of wine a day is good for our hearts, they then informed us that this is not so, and any alcohol is bad for us, and if you drink more than two standard alcoholic drinks a day it could lead to cancer or heart failure. Now I see where they've changed their minds again and it's back in favour. God help the racing and footy fraternity, they don't know where they are.

If you're under twenty you're a 'binge drinker' and if you're over forty, you're an alcoholic. I always refer to myself as a binge drinker; it makes me feel younger. Over the years I've noticed that if you wait long enough, expert opinions change like the wind. I'm waiting for them to discover that smoking is good for your nervous system. After all, my mother-in-law was prescribed smoking by her doctor in Cairns while Marie's father was away in New Guinea during the war.

Yet television is obsessed with food and cooking programs. We have to read the infinitesimal writing on the labels of everything we buy to make sure the evil manufacturers aren't trying to poison us, and yet sometimes the experts are giving us inexpert advice! It seems to me, if you eat a half-ton serving of anything it could be carcinogenic or fattening or aging, or all three. And if you're a fat, old, petrol-sniffing, drug-taking, gay Aboriginal carnivore, you're really in deep shit.

Her physical limitations are appallingly frustrating for her, but she tries again and again and seldom complains. It's something you never consider until you have no option. Only having the use of one arm and needing a walking stick to maintain her balance is severely restricting. She can't even make a cup of tea and carry it to a table without help.

She used to be an excellent cook and really enjoyed it. She still cooks occasionally, propping herself against the kitchen bench, but she needs me there as kitchen hand and apprentice chef to fetch and carry, measure ingredients and cut things up, carry the baking tins to the oven, and get them out when they're cooked, and wash and clean up afterwards; all of the things that need two hands. Together we have three so we manage.

Forget the meat-and-three-veg dinners we were brought up on. Now it has to be Greek or Italian, Eastern or Turkish or any other bloody nationality's food. I must admit I haven't seen a program yet on the delights of Ugandan cooking or Tasty Tid Bits from Tanzania. Maybe they wouldn't appeal to the Western palate. And have you noticed that everything has to include chilli nowadays? It's the big flavour *de jour*: chilli sauce, chilli salad, and chilli ice cream. It's sure to burn out any cancer or colon problem. And we take vitamin supplements for everything. Among the one hundred and fifty other packets and bottles of tablets in our drug drawer, we take glucosamine for our joints, Prosqn for my prostate, and fish oil for our brains and memory, but half the time I can't remember where I've put them. And I get a sore back, swollen knees and a pain in the ass, bending down to open the drawer.

I have a friend who was raised entirely on Vegemite sandwiches; it's all she would eat. Her mother would serve her meat and three veg, and as soon as the caring mother turned her back, whatever was on the plate would be chucked out the kitchen window. Yet my friend has grown into a very fit and healthy sixty-year-old woman. Years later when their house was sold, the new owners called in a team of archaeologists to study the graveyard of bones they'd discovered in the back yard. It turned out it wasn't the remains of dinosaurs as they'd suspected; it was pork and lamb chops.

Enough of this. We've got to have something to look forward to. We've got to do something to prove that our lives aren't entirely over yet. We've often talked about taking a cruise somewhere. That way we will only have to pack and unpack at the beginning and end of the voyage. The South Pacific would be the obvious choice but their shore excursions seem to have some tendered transfers and the emphasis seems to be on lots of white, coral sand beaches, snorkelling and diving or other energetic excursions, which are really out of our league now. Must check with the travel agents.

Speaking of food: what on earth is wrong with Genetically Modified food? Most of the stuff we eat has genetically modified itself over the centuries anyway. A carrot, apple or slice of steak is not in the same genetic composition it was originally. Surely genetically modifying food to allow for feeding the rapidly increasing population of the world would be desirable. It's not as if it has to be done by adding chemicals and hormones.

And why does 'organic' food cost so much more than inorganic? I mean, think of the money they save on pesticides and chemically enhanced fertilisers. If you're that way inclined, what about permaculture? All you need is a few newspapers, a pile of straw, a slosh of water and a heap of shit, which sounds a lot like life really.

I am continually amazed at how much people apparently eat. When I go to the supermarket I am confronted by queues of people with trolleys piled high with enough food to last a family of ten for a month. The supermarkets are now open seven days a week, and yet it looks like everybody is expecting a famine to strike overnight.

And what is frightening is the unhealthy variety of stuff they load into their trolleys: cartons of Coke; boxes of potato chips; a variety of sweets and nibbles; ice creams; huge economy-size packs of toilet paper; jars and packets of processed sauces and pre-prepared meals; detergents and cleaning agents full of oil-based ingredients to kill our waterways; frozen meals; and maybe one pack of frozen mixed vegetables. So much for the nutritionists and food gurus. And why do we have to have a detergent to wash our clothes and some other ingredient to take out any stains? I thought that's what detergent was supposed to do?

Despite the mind-boggling number of cooking programs on television, nobody seems to cook now days, except me and Nigella. They could get rid of Master Chef and all those foodie shows as long as they kept the lovely Nigella, and that's got nothing to do with what she cooks. When She Who Can't Be Ignored decides she wants to cook, I debase myself and take off my chef's hat and slip into my role as Kitchen Hand Extraordinaire, and our cooking sessions soon turn into an episode of Gordon Ramsay's *Hell's Kitchen*.

> She: Have you sealed the meat before you put it in the casserole?

Me: Yes, dear.

She: And the vegetables?

Me: Yes, dear.

She: Will you cut this up for me?

Me: Yes, dear.

She: And hold this for me.

Me: Yes, dear.

She: And get the flour out of the pantry, and the sugar and the butter from the fridge, and while you're there get me the eggs and the milk. Will you wipe that oil up you dropped on the floor; my walking stick might slip on it. Where's the jug I was using?

Me: I washed it.

She: I haven't finished using it yet.

Me: Sorry, dear.

She: What herbs have you put in the casserole?

Me: Only the sage, cumin, garlic, thyme, tarragon, oregano, coriander, paprika, cardamom, rosemary, and a hint of Moroccan.

Her: What? I told you all I wanted was basil! Didn't you read the recipe?

Me: I like to be a bit creative.

Her: I know your sense of being creative. Curry powder in a butter sponge cake does not go!

Me: I thought it would give an interesting Indian flavour: Especially with the cumin in the icing.

Her: Sponge cakes are NOT Indian!

Me (sighing): Fuckin' purist!

I remember one of our son's ex-girlfriends, one of the interchangeable blondes that continuously haunted the place, trying to ingratiate herself into She Who Can't Be Ignored's good books one day, by offering to help her bake a cake. So out came the flour, eggs, sugar and the rest of the fifty ingredients absolutely essential for baking a delectable artery-blocker, and The Interchangeable Blonde looked positively askance. 'But where's the box of cake mix?' she mewed. 'You can't bake a cake without the box of cake mix.'

'I *never* use cake mix,' was the contemptuous reply. She doesn't either; she uses one of the four thousand recipes she's religiously collected since we were married, and which are stored in a series of cupboards, drawers, shelves and a large tin trunk in the garage. 'For this particular *gateau*,' she says, 'I always use a recipe handed down through countless generations of Scottish ancestors. The original creator was raped and pillaged by English soldiers whilst escaping across the Highlands with Bonnie Prince Charlie.'

'But the recipe is on the cake-mix box, silly,' says the Interchangeable Blonde.

A sneer from She Who Mustn't Be Advised, and another blossoming relationship shot to hell.

New Zealand it is! Booked a passage on the Sapphire Princess. *It departs from Sydney on the 14th of February for a twelve-night cruise to Auckland. We're very excited, as we've never been to New Zealand. Much to do.*

Chapter 15

I gird my shrinking loins for the supermarket, put on my prescription, bottle-top glasses and get out my pocket Webster's Dictionary to try to read and understand the Nutrition Information labels to see how much salt, sugar, preservatives, colouring and other life-threatening chemicals they contain, only to find I need another magnifying glass as well as my glasses to read the minute printing on the list of ingredients.

Having made my purchases, I then grope my way to the check-out counter, because I've forgotten to take off the glasses, to be confronted by a queue of twenty over-laden trolleys, with plump women guarding them like Masai tribeswomen at a UN Food Relief drop, while at the same time, leafing through this week's *Woman's Day*, or some other 'celebrity' rag, to fill in the waiting time. Their small children, like a pack of pitiful, clawing refugees, scream for Chupa Chups or strategically placed eye-catching sweets, or demand to be taken to the toilet, which, of course, is thoughtfully situated on the other side of the check-out counter and probably a block away.

When I finally manage to run over a few small feet and sideswipe a few obese bums with my trolley and get to the checkout, I find it's become automated! Yet another computerised monster of buttons to push and slots to insert your credit cards or Fly-buys, and a patronising, sugary, computerised voice ordering me around like some sweet-talking Gestapo guard in Belsen. You can't argue or complain about prices or quality with a computer. And there is absolutely no satisfaction in saying 'Oh, fuck off, computer lady!' because all she says is, 'Have a nice day, and thank you for shopping at We'll Rip You Off Supermarket.'

When I finally escape the interrogation, I am forced to search for my car in the car park because some unqualified bastard has parked in the Fuckin' Cripple Parking space, and I see this cute young thing coming toward me and go into the pick-up line that never fails: 'Excuse me, my dear, but could you direct me to the Swallow's Nest Retirement Village?' I say with a vulnerable smile, just this side of a leer.

'Of course,' she says, in what I choose to take as a provocative manner. 'It's a hundred metres down the street there. You can't miss it. It's the one with the twenty-foot-high, electrified, razor-wire fence. Are you visiting your mother?'

Sweet-talking she-devil, I think.

'No, I know it's hard to believe, but I live there. I just forgot where it was.'

'Well, you'd better take off those bottle top glasses or you'll never find it. And by the way, I'm a bloke.'

Oh well, at my age you can't be too fussy.

We seem to spend a lot of time looking for clothes for the trip. She's almost obsessed with the way she looks now. No matter how much I try to reassure her, she still worries about not looking like a 'normal' person, as she puts it. She even makes sure she's wearing her makeup and is dressed as well as she can be when we go to the supermarket or shopping mall. I admire her enormously for her pride and determination but she now has such low esteem and self-confidence since the stroke. She always took care of her appearance before and dressed beautifully and mixed with people easily. Now she feels self-conscious and unsure of herself in a group of people and tries to avoid crowds. I guess it's very understandable under the circumstances. She says she doesn't want me to be ashamed of her. As if I could be. She's been so courageous and strong and will always be beautiful to me.

Whatever happened to the checkout chicks – the young people who couldn't get a part-time job anywhere else, or those middle-aged wives trying to help out with the mortgage repayments or pay off the Audi? I do miss them. I loved the way they used to recite, in one breath, ignoring any full stops or commas, the under-rehearsed script the management gave them: 'Hello-how-are-you-today-I'm-fine-thank-you-any-Fly-buys?-credit-or-debit-any-cash-out?' And after they'd packed your groceries they'd say, 'Have a nice day' in a flat, unsmiling and insincere voice.

I always wanted to say, 'I'll try, but I'm an eighty-year-old pensioner with a terminal disease, so I've got other plans.' But I don't think it would even register.

I think I got a bit carried away with the idea of cruising. I've always wanted to do a Mediterranean cruise and Marie's always dreamed of visiting Egypt. I had a bit of a chat with the travel agent and it just so happened that he'd received that very day, would you believe, this super special email deal for a return cruise from Rome to Istanbul, with a full-day shore excursion in Alexandria where we could get to Cairo to see the Pyramids and Cairo Museum, departing in early November.

We have put some money aside for a trip after I retire and God knows, I'm ready to retire and the stock market is looking very healthy ... Oh, what the hell, let's go for it.

Chapter 16

After the supermarket debacle, you then have to face the bloody school pick-up or drop-off traffic that holds you up for an extra hour on a good day. If they must, why don't parents drop the kids off at the nearest bus stop or train station and pick them up there after school? At least that might unclog some of the streets in a twenty-kilometre radius around the bloody schools. Or why can't the older kids ride a bike, or heaven forbid, walk?

When I went to school I had to walk bare-footed for two miles on a track through the bush. One of my mates, whose parents were even poorer, didn't even have much in the proper bare feet department. And on the way home we used to stop and fish for yabbies in the creek or I'd have a bit of a pash with the cute little girl who sat in the back row of my classroom. If I was an hour late home my mother wouldn't fret and ring the police or the SAS; she'd say, 'That little bugger's either fishing for yabbies in the creek or having a pash with the cute little girl who sits in the back row of his classroom.'

Nowadays, with the media-hyped fear, and the amount of child pornography on the web, the paedophiles have really come out of the closet, and we're led to believe there's at least one on every corner with a bag of boiled lollies at the ready.

Which reminds me, if China can block out websites about Tibet or anything else they don't want the public to see, why can't we block out websites that contain child pornography?

In all those years of walking through the bush I wasn't once accosted by a paedophile. Mind you, I was a rather unattractive kid.

And God save me from those little trainee people of today who are dressed up like dolls in their cute, exorbitantly priced, little designer label outfits. If I had more than one pair of shorts, a shirt or two and a pair of sandals, I was considered flashy and overdressed.

We've become so brainwashed by the legion of yet more 'experts' on cleanliness, the little kids of today are constantly disinfected and kept so hygienically clean and germ free they may as well be hermetically packed and sealed like everything else. We're lowering their immune system and not building up their natural resistance to infections, diseases and asthma. Of course, that all changes when they become teenagers. We're quite happy to allow their minds to be polluted with crime and violence. Come on, kids, 'Get a Little Dirt On Your Hands' instead of your minds. Kids today are so protected they aren't getting the street skills they will need to survive in the real world of adulthood, or adultery.

Now there are so many families with both parents working to pay the mortgage and over-extended credit cards, and, of course, to maintain at least two cars, one of which must be the obligatory off-road, four-wheel drive specifically designed for picking up and delivering school kids. And then we have the one hundred other 'necessities', like Nintendo games, overseas trips, school excursions to the Bahamas and beauty treatments for their four-year-old daughters.

On top of this, the long-suffering parents are also forced to pay for after-school care or activities to 'improve their children's potential', which is mainly an excuse to keep the kids off the streets and occupied while the parents are both working. The plethora of diversions include among many others, Speech and Drama, or Acting For The Screen, self defence, music, ballet, Mandarin for five year olds, Accountancy and Business Law for Kids and in some extreme Muslim schools, 'How to build Your own Bomb'. We're turning our youth into Chinese-speaking, reality-television performers who can negotiate their own contracts while moonlighting as terrorists.

I hope I've arranged everything: clothes; toiletries; Marie's makeup; prescription drugs to last the time we're away; portable bed post and over-toilet seat; passports and travel documents; transfers to and from the ports; a waterproof under-blanket in case of emergency; and a luxury hotel for the cat. (He thinks he's sending us away on the cruise to be looked after while he has a break in the Meowiatt Spa and Retreat.)

I'm sure I've forgotten something. This is all a bit scary; it's so different from our other overseas trips. But hey, you know the old adage that has become my mantra: just get off your ass and do it.

Chapter 17

What's all this Equality of the Sexes bullshit? As far as I'm concerned women have always been superior to men. Why would they want to change that? Why would they want to be 'equal' and force their way into what were formerly male domains? I can't understand why women would insist on being allowed to enter vulgar, loud-mouthed, gambling, drinking, swearing, sweating, farting, smoke-filled (well, they used to be before women were allowed) bars and other dens of iniquity, quite unsuitable for the fairer sex and the mothers of our innocent children. Smoking was fairly acceptable, or at least tolerated, in the company of other men, probably because a lot of fellas didn't like being called Wowser Poof Wankers by the then smoking male majority.

Did the women think they were missing out on something? Did they want to check up on us? It's a male thing. It's all right to have women's secret business so why not men's? Men aren't queuing up to chain themselves to the railings of the CWA, but it is true some of them do slip into breast-feeding classes.

On the other side of the coin, I was talking to a woman the other day who was a member of the fairly well-known Red Hat Club. For those who aren't familiar with this particular club, it is a group of women who attend gatherings, luncheons and other social events, ostensibly for charity, but I suspect to outshine the other women dressed in red hats. She told me that a couple of gay guys applied to join and their membership was refused! I don't know if they were given a reason for the refusal but I suspect that the gay guys probably looked swishier in their hats, and had better accessories than the other battle-axes in the club.

You seldom hear of a woman being accused of sexual harassment because most men wouldn't mind being sexually harassed. At my age I'd welcome it. But I have never heard of a woman politician being accused of chair sniffing. Of course women should be allowed equal rights and pay. Of course they should be allowed to be business leaders or lawyers or politicians or whatever they want to be. (Mind you, Margaret Thatcher put a dent in that argument.) And being a good mother is a pretty important full-time occupation if you ask me and should be paid for as such, by the tax payers if necessary. Maybe then the kids would have more home life and a lot of our youth wouldn't be so violent and uncontrollable.

A few of the extreme 'women's liberationists' or feminists of the seventies gave the whole movement a bad name with men. Burning your bra may be symbolic but it sure gives you saggy bosoms and charred nipples, especially if you don't take the bra off first. It did tend to make it look like it wasn't equality they were demanding but superiority. But it left men unsure of their position in society. You can't blame them. I like men; they're less complex and straight forward. The alpha male position had been what they'd aspired to for centuries and here were their 'little' women standing up for equality and threatening that position. Of course men reacted. It de-balled them.

And in a lot of ways women suffered for it. Men are very physical beings and if they lose their self-esteem they feel threatened and some are easily brought to violence and lash out with disastrous results. Now I'm shocked to see on television and web postings, a growing number of young girls and women out of control with alcohol and drugs, fighting in the streets or schoolyards, or staggering out of a nightclub and spewing on the footpath, a thing I never experienced when I was young. How can they expect to be treated with respect?

The first hiccup happens when the limo I'd arranged and paid for to take us from Mascot Airport to the Cruise Terminal at Circular Quay turns out to be a forty-seater coach! I mention I'd hired and paid for a limo and not a school bus to the driver and he says, 'Sorry mate, I'm just going by the instructions from the office. Get in.' Well, we eventually manage to get Marie up the steps of the coach and into one of the front seats where we sit in solitary splendour, just the two of us, in this huge coach, as we are driven to the port.

The service to check in and board is excellent and the staff are very helpful. The large disabled cabin with its own private balcony is wonderful and everything we could hope for. So far so good.

Chapter 18

Now it is probably true that when you start to look like your passport photograph, you really do need a holiday. Travelling with someone in a wheelchair does present certain challenges and cruising is one of them. But experience is a wonderful thing because it helps me to recognise my mistakes when I make them again. We did two cruises in one year. The first ship, the *Sapphire Princess*, was huge and of course most of the indoor area was laid with carpet. It was like pushing a wheelchair the full length of a football field that had been fertilised and overgrown with weeds, and of course, I never knew where I was or which way I was going or which was port, starboard, fore or aft.

The 'Abandon Ship' exercise we all had to attend after boarding was a bit of a hoot. We all had to congregate in various lounges for instructions as to what we were to do in case of an emergency. After we went through the long procedure we were then told that disabled passengers were to stay in their cabins and wait for crew assistance. I could just imagine the ship going down like the *Titanic*, and the crew screaming, 'Fuck the cripples, I'm outta here!'

I did learn pretty quickly which was the port side, because that was the side where you were allowed to smoke. It wasn't easy working out which direction the ship was travelling though and I was constantly peering out through windows to get my bearings, or asking members of the crew, or other confused passengers wandering the corridors with perplexed expressions and a map of the ship clutched in their trembling fingers.

I've always had a rather romantic idea of cruising, no doubt fuelled by the old Hollywood movies: wealthy, attractive guests dressed to perfection, the ladies in beautiful outfits with hats, shoes and stockings, and the men in tailored suits or smart casual wear, straight out of *Esquire* magazine, promenading the decks or relaxing in deckchairs with hardback novels and exotic, frangipani-decorated drinks. Marie looked for Fred and Ginger: Fred dressed impeccably in an immaculate dinner suit and Ginger in a wonderful flowing gown gliding around the polished dance floor to the strains of Glenn Miller and his fifty-piece orchestra, cocktails or Champagne on the deck and stolen chaste kisses bathed in the silvery moonlight. Dinners at the captain's table with plates of food that looked more like works of art, accompanied by carefully selected wines, polite laughter and witty, sophisticated, Noel Coward type conversation. If they were ever like that, how things have changed.

Instead of Jane Powell and Debbie Reynolds we got Edith Evans and Wilfred Hyde-White. The glamorous gay young things adorning the colourful brochures were certainly in the minority. Or if they were on board at all, they must've been hidden away in their cabins, rooting or recuperating from a heavy night of booze and drugs in the Sky Walker nightclub. The over-fifty brigade majority were more inclined to be slopping around in thongs, clod-hopping sandals or grubby runners and shapeless sports gear, stuffing their jowled faces with cream cakes and other goodies from the Horizon smörgåsbord. On the three 'formal dress' evenings they suddenly hatched from their cocoons and metamorphosed into glamorous evening wear, usually black with beads and glitter, and played at being sophisticated. It's all so pretentious. Whatever happened to natural style?

On the first cruise we called in at Melbourne and visited old friends then spent a couple of days crossing Bass Strait, which behaved itself, thank God, then Hobart, with a visit to Mount Wellington and a view from the summit which was clouded in as usual. Then it was on to New Zealand, across the sometimes treacherous Tasman Sea. One of the crew told us on the previous return trip from Auckland they'd run into a hurricane with thirty-foot waves! That would've been nice. I could just imagine pushing She Who Doesn't Get Seasick uphill and downhill in a wheelchair, dodging flying crockery, overturned furniture and the odd projectile 'barf'.

My God! Waking up on a dazzling morning and breakfasting on croissants, coffee and fresh fruit on your own private balcony, looking out at your first sight of Milford Sound, at the most southern tip of New Zealand, is breathtaking! The shining, calm, blue-green water, with a backdrop of soaring mountains and cliffs of verdant green, slashed with the scars of landslides and waterfalls, is absolutely stunning. From time to time, fishing boats appeared, miniscule in the distance, cutting their way through the crystal water. The sense of peacefulness was sublime.

But why oh why do they have to leave trolleys of linen, cleaning equipment and bathroom toiletries parked unattended in the ship's corridors and blocking the poor bastards trying to push someone in a wheelchair? And sometimes you have to take the elevator up or down a couple of decks and walk a mile to be able to get from one end of the bloody ship to the other.

At Port Chalmers, the port for Dunedin, we did a trip to Larnach Castle; not what you'd call wheelchair-friendly, but with help we managed. Not a bad excursion but the Devonshire morning tea was the hit as far as I was concerned.

Thought Christchurch a bit ordinary but, to be fair, we did go on the ship's shore excursion that took us through only the main streets of town. The coach driver rabbited on, pointing out the various landmarks: 'And now we're passing through the more exclusive part of town. You'll notice the expensive homes along the way. Some of them are selling for over a million dollars!'

I think the buyers were robbed. They should've bought on the Gold Coast. No earthquakes there.

The final destination was a local farm, a 'top tourist spot' that stocked Alpacas and other exotic breeds. The farm was pretty run down with uneven rutted dirt paths and we couldn't get the wheelchair up to see the Alpacas in the distant paddock. I tried and nearly ruptured myself in the process. The toilets were out of order so the forty-odd passengers had to cope with a couple of small Porta Loos. They are NOT Fuckin' Cripple Friendly. Finally managed to squeeze my loved one in but had to hold the door open and stand guard outside. Most of the men found a tree to piss up against. There are definitely strong advantages in being a man.

The obligatory Devonshire tea saved me from an exhausted tantrum, but the gift shop, a single room filled with stuffed kiwis (the bird variety), sheep (what else?), koalas and kangaroos (now that was original), all made in China, sent us scurrying back to the coach to rest my aching back and legs.

After twelve days at sea we finally reached Auckland for disembarkation. Wouldn't you know it would fuckin' rain! Getting off the ship was bearable but finding our luggage was a nightmare. Finally got out to the taxi rank to find the taxi I'd booked and paid for months earlier had left with another fare! I rang the taxi company in high dudgeon and was told they'd send another one, so I wait in the rain with a leaking umbrella, a wet wife, in a wet wheelchair, and wet suitcases; a lovely end to the cruise!

They booked us in quickly at the Hyatt reception because it wouldn't look good for their image having a soaking, bedraggled, cripple in a soaking wheelchair running water like she'd wet herself, with suitcases dripping water onto their expensive carpets, and me standing there like the Grumpy Ancient Mariner.

So much for the room with disabled facilities we had been assured of when booking. The shower was over a bloody high bath! What is wrong with these people? If you can't walk, how are you going to get your leg over a bathtub? It looked like She Who Can't Get Her Leg Up was going to be She Who Can't Be Showered, so she just had to cope with the famous 'armpit, crotch and bum wash.' Thank God we were only there for two nights.

I asked the concierge at the hotel if he could recommend an Asian or Thai restaurant for dinner, which he did. He rang and booked a table for us and verified it was wheelchair-friendly.

That night, when the taxi dropped us off down town, outside the restaurant, we discovered the restaurant was on the first floor with no elevator in sight. Leaving my loved one alone on the pavement, and I felt sure, highly likely to be accosted by some passing Maori street gang, I hurried up the stairs to confront the smiling Chinese receptionist. 'No worries,' she said, 'I will send someone down to help you.' She then dispatched two huge Oriental-type Maoris to carry my fragile one in the wheelchair, upstairs and into the restaurant.

She Who Hates Being Carried In A Wheelchair finally gave in to their insistence, despite the fact that it makes her feel very noticeable and insecure. The smart-ass bearers wanted to know if I wanted to be carried up too. With great aplomb and dignity, I declined. But I was tempted. So much for wheelchair-friendly. Well, they did smile and chat, I suppose, as they puffed their way up the flight of twenty-odd stairs.

The next day we visited the Sky Tower, which was impressive, and then I decided, in a lightheaded moment, to head back to Queen Street, which from the taxi drive into town, looked like one of the few flat streets in the city. To get there we had to wheel down the side of a fuckin' mountain!

With my loved one riding the brake, and me in serious danger of a double hernia, and putting pedestrians in grave danger of being flattened by a runaway wheelchair, we zigzagged our way down the mountain, with the minimum amount of screaming, and finally came to a nerve-wracking stop, relatively unscathed but breathing heavily for all the wrong reasons.

Air New Zealand served us a meat pie on the flight back to Brisbane. Whether that was for lunch or just a snack, I can't remember because, unlike my usual style, I got myself into a bit of a flap. Just after the pie was served, I suddenly discovered to my horror that my passport was missing! I rummaged through the leather document case, searched my pockets, and looked on the seat and floor to no avail. My mild agitation was noticed by a very 'happy' steward who asked what my problem was.

'I've lost my friggin' passport!' I almost screamed hysterically.

Obviously used to grey-haired Withereds, he calmly said, 'Now don't get yourself excited, dear,' a phrase that is guaranteed to have the opposite effect, 'You must've had it when you came on board, silly. Have you checked all your pockets, love?'

'Of course I've checked my bloody pockets, darling,' I yelled as I flapped my hands over my new, cream-coloured cargo pants again, like I was beating out a bush fire.

Shock, horror, oops! I giggled self-consciously. 'Here it is in my pants leg pocket. How the hell did it get there? Sorry, mate,' I apologised gruffly, in my most masculine manner.

He smiled in what can only be described as a patronising manner, and minced off to attend to another passenger. Greatly relieved, I flopped back into my seat, only to find that I'd inadvertently placed my pie there while searching for my passport. I immediately jumped to my feet again, feeling a warm, damp sensation spreading around the circumference of my anus. I looked like I'd shit myself! And the spreading dollop of tomato sauce made it look even more serious.

When we eventually got home we picked the mongrel cat up from the luxury spa resort, and he berated me for the next week, complaining that we'd left him in a bloody cheap 'cattery'! He went on about the lousy, two-star accommodation, and the food you wouldn't serve to a dog, let alone a pedigreed feline of Egyptian ancestry, and complained about the low class of the other 'inmates' he'd been forced to socialise with in the 'concentration camp'. I didn't dare mention the Mediterranean cruise later in the year but I think he was a bit suspicious because he sat on my desk while I was on the web and growled at the websites for hotel accommodation and limo hire in Rome. In high dudgeon, he poked his paw at the references to 'No Pets Allowed', and tried to eat my mouse.

> *In spite of occasional hiccups, the New Zealand trip has been a huge success and, best of all, Marie has had a wonderful time. I'm so proud of her and the way she's coped. Now we've tried it and learned a few lessons about travelling in our situation, we feel much more confident about the Mediterranean cruise later in the year.*
>
> *We've decided on a different cruise, which leaves a bit later in autumn, a much better time in Europe. This one travels the Eastern Mediterranean but doesn't call into Alexandria, so we decide to spend ten days in Egypt before we fly home. This is turning into a marathon but, hey, it's another adventure to look forward to.*
>
> *After ten months of planning I've done the best I can. Airline tickets and hotels are booked in Rome, Cairo, Luxor and Dubai and private limos are booked for the shore excursions on the cruise because we have difficulty using coaches. This will probably be our last overseas trip so we intend to make the most of it.*

We're leaving for the cruise from Civitavecchia, the port of Rome. Both of us are really excited about the cruise and returning to Rome again for a few days prior to the cruise and can talk of little else. We remember being there in 1999 on our last trip, three months before Marie had the stroke, and we had a wonderful time. We stayed a couple of weeks in a private villa in Chianti, in the magnificent Tuscan countryside, and explored Florence and Venice. It was the most marvellous trip. We walked and drove everywhere. Thank God we did it then.

Having a bit of discomfort with my left hip and thigh but the X-rays show nothing wrong with the replacement. Probably just a muscle strain from all the packing and preparation. A couple of weeks' rest on the ship should fix it.

Chapter 19

Some of my friends asked me if I was worried about terrorism on the trip. Why would I worry? I've been married for nearly fifty years. We flew Emirates Business Class and the airline ticket included a limo pick-up and delivery between home and the airport, and limo transfers from airport to our hotel in Rome. For the price they charge they should include a case of Bollinger and the cruise fares!

It was the first time we'd flown Business Class and, as they say, it's the only way to fly. But bloody hell! Every time we landed for fuel or cleaning we had to get off the plane and take our hand luggage with us, go through security, race to an allocated, uncivilised smoking area for a quick drag, belt back to the departure lounge and go through the security screening again (!) and back on the plane, and all in the space of under a couple of hours. With a wheelchair, even with passenger assist, this is NOT recommended. Why all the security checks in the airport for a couple of hours' stopover? I mean you're not likely to pick up a bomb or a supply of drugs, or an AK-74M from Duty Free, are you?

These enforced stopovers happened in Singapore, Dubai and Milan and really pissed me off. At least we were more comfortable in Business Class than the poor wretches in Economy, and apart from the fuel stops and minuscule toilets, which certainly weren't Fuckin' Cripple-Friendly, I almost enjoyed the long twenty-six-hour flight for the first time in my life.

Arriving in Rome again was such a thrill. The passenger assist and the limo trip to the delightful Hotel Della Muse, in the outer Parioli district, were all we could hope for. It was a greener area where a lot of Embassies are located. We hadn't visited this side of Rome before and it was truly lovely. The hotel room and friendly, helpful staff were perfect for our needs and there was a very quiet, attractive, vine-covered courtyard, dining and garden area just a short distance from our room. The room itself was more than adequate and actually equipped for the disabled with a large stand-up shower cubicle in the en suite as promised.

After my exhausting experience with pushing the wheelchair all over the bloody *Sapphire Princess* on the last cruise, I managed, with no small difficulty I might add, to pre-book a portable electric wheelchair in Rome for this cruise. The only company I could find on the web who would agree to hire the chair didn't have an English-speaking staff member so I cleverly arranged with the English-speaking limo driver I'd booked to drive us over and pick it up the day after we arrived, and drive us on to the Musei Capitolini Galleries for a bit of a look around and lunch afterwards.

Our driver's name was Enzo, a charming, distinguished, seventy-eight-year-old gentleman whose main claim to fame (which he often mentioned) was having been a chauffeur for 'Royalty', which made me feel like some tired old queen. After a quick whiz past the Spanish Steps, which we hadn't seen on our last trip, and which looked for all the world like a flight of stone steps to me, we arrived at some small medical supply company to pick up the portable chair.

Well, I suppose you could call it 'portable' if you happened to have a five-ton truck and two large Latinos with a forklift to assist, but I must admit I had my doubts about getting it into Enzo's medium-sized five-door SUV. As expected, with my extensive vocabulary in Italian, which was pretty well exhausted after *grazie*, *buongiorno*, *arrivederci*, *cappuccino* and the internationally recognised *fuck off*, I did have the slightest difficulty in understanding the instructions, even with the assistance of Enzo's heavily accented English. After much jocularity, gestures, arm waving, frowning and loud bilingual intercourse, they somehow managed to dissect the wheelchair into three separate parts, each part weighing at least half a ton, and with the help of the two ex-gladiator assistants, squeeze it into the back of the van, which left me in a rather cramped foetal position with my head jammed between a side window and a hard black heavy tread wheelchair tyre.

Off we went to the Capitolini and with the grateful assistance of a couple of passing friendly Carmelite nuns, who were built like the Colosseum, we unloaded and reassembled the 'portable' wheelchair and sent Enzo on his way to his next appointment (with Royalty no doubt), saying confidently we'd get a taxi back to the hotel.

The Capitolini Galleries were very interesting and the Michelangelo-designed piazza that surrounded them was spectacular. We had a magnificent lunch on the rooftop terrace overlooking the dome of St Peter's and the spectacular rooftops of Rome, with no thought of the cost until the bill arrived and I, quite uncontrollably, exclaimed in shock, and possibly just a fraction too loudly, 'Fuck!' to which the waiter, quick as a flash, replied, 'That would cost you another one hundred Euro, signor, but my mother she is very clean.'

As we prepared to leave before I bought the rest of the building, I suddenly discovered to my horror that even with the brake off, the wheelchair wouldn't move of its own accord! I quickly tried to remember the instructions I'd been given in broken English, but came to the conclusion, based on my innate sense of mechanics and technical ability, that the battery must've flattened while we were having lunch!

I managed to push, pull and curse the chair down a steep incline and back to the piazza, where I rang the hotel to tell them of my plight and asked them to ring the supplier and ask them to send a mechanic, which, because of the language problem, I couldn't do. They said to ring back in ten minutes and they'd tell me what was happening. Suddenly the piazza and the Capitolini lost their charm as we sat and waited.

After ten minutes I rang the hotel again and they said, 'The mechanic says, have you lifted the bar on the side of the chair that puts it in drive?' Oops! She Who Can't Be Ignored must've knocked the bar during lunch and disconnected the drive.

'*Grazie bella*, Mr Hotel Manager,' I blurted out in relief as She Who Suddenly Remembered re-engaged the drive of the wheelchair and sniggering evilly at my lack of mechanical prowess, slowly started to weave across the piazza, dodging tourists and heading straight towards Michelangelo's famous flight of stairs that led to the street below. I was so tempted to let her go but I finally relented and limped painfully after her muttering to myself, 'Remember, you promised unconditional love.'

Now it's simple to get a taxi in Rome at peak hours, isn't it? You simply stand in the road with your hand up and they run over your foot. Gregory Peck did it in *Roman Holiday*. Well, he did have Audrey Hepburn with him. I was accompanied by an old blonde in a tank. We had to find a *maxima volumi* taxi; that is, a big bastard.

To do this we had to walk for fuckin' miles past the Forum, and cross roads with drivers intent on maiming their quota of tourists for the day, trying several taxis along the way which were too small, before we were eventually taken pity on by a wonderful young taxi driver who, it turned out, had relatives in Melbourne (of course), and with the help of a few heavily muscled, taxi-driver-charioteer mates, finally got the chair into the back of his cab and took us back to the hotel.

But what an adventure it was being back in Rome. Just to see the Colosseum, to walk the Forum and the Sistine Chapel and discover again the ruins that appear around almost every corner. To eat the delicious food, and sit drinking a cappuccino or a glass of wine in a piazza, and watch the passing parade of locals and tourists clutching maps, to soak in the atmosphere was truly wonderful. We were a bit limited in just how much we could do this time and the cobbled streets and wheelchair access were a bit of a problem, but we found the help we got from the friendly Italians and the other tourists was amazing.

Sunday in the Borghese Gardens and the Museo was delightful; the families at play, strolling and picnicking on the manicured lawns, licking delicious gelato, pedalling bicycles, chatting and laughing. The Galleria Borghese with its magnificent architecture, paintings and sculptures was breathtaking. How good it was to be back.

The drive up to the Tivoli gardens, just outside Rome, was shithouse. It seems every large city in the world has its dreary side. Traffic was heavy but Enzo managed well. I suppose, driving Royalty around made him used to barging his way through traffic and expecting to have right of way, and Marie constantly giving the Royal wave probably helped.

To avoid Enzo suffering another hernia, we took the manual wheelchair this time, which meant we couldn't get around much in Tivoli itself as the cobbled lanes are narrow, steep and winding and we had to be satisfied with seeing it from the car. But it looked picturesque, and the fountains in the gardens at the Villa d'Este are magnificent.. Enzo opted for a toilet break, no doubt to relieve his prostate enlargement condition and catch up with the locals, so we were driven around the gardens in an electric golf buggy, which is available for disabled tourists. Got lost on the way out of the villa of course, which meant pushing the wheelchair an extra mile trying to find the right bloody elevator or risk being entombed in the Villa D'Este.

My leg is still giving me a bit of a problem but I'm sure it will improve when we get on the ship. Marie is holding up brilliantly and seems to be enjoying herself, but the old vivacity is gone. I know she feels the excitement inside but it just doesn't show as much as it used to.

Last time we were in Italy, she came down with what was diagnosed later as a viral pneumonia but I now suspect it was Legionnaires disease. This was just before we were to leave for home and she had great difficulty with her breathing and walking. It was touch and go that they would allow her to fly but we insisted and they eventually relented.

It came on very quickly the day we took a coach tour from Rome to Pompeii. She was so weak she couldn't walk through the ruins and had to suffer a fourteen-hour day in the coach before we could return to the hotel and get a doctor.

Several hundred dollars and two doctors later – thank God for travel insurance – a couple of antibiotic scripts, and an overnight train from Rome to Vienna, they finally agreed to let her fly home. Stupidly not thinking about an airport wheelchair, I pushed her through the Vienna airport on a luggage trolley to the departure gate. At least this time we have our own wheelchair. So far her health has been good. Let's hope that continues.

The *Galaxy*, for the Med cruise, was a slightly smaller ship than the last cruise and we did have the portable electric wheelchair on board this time. We had a nice large disabled cabin, but no private balcony, which was a shame. Again, a bit like a floating Billy Butlin's Holiday Camp For The Over-Fifties, so we felt at home. Still couldn't find Fred or Ginger though. Just as well they missed the boat because they would've stood out in that crowd. I think it was the same mob that travelled with us on the *Sapphire Princess*. They sure dressed the same.

They didn't have Anytime Dining on this ship and we were allocated to a second sitting in the enormous, one-thousand-seat dining room. It was all very swish I suppose and the service was the usual five star, but we agreed the food was more three star in quality. It was very disappointing for us septuagenarian food connoisseurs. Nothing was vitamised!

On top of that, the second sitting didn't sit until 8:45pm. By the time we got to the main course we were nodding off into the *coq au vin*! Of course we had the obligatory formal night dress-ups, which were a bit of a pain, but by God we looked good in our finery, slumped over the table, fast asleep.

The lateness of the dinner meant that the stage shows in the theatre were so full by the time we got there, we couldn't get a seat because all the seats at the back for the disabled had been taken.

The casino turned out to be as profitable as the last ship, which was zilch, so we wandered the decks or tried to get a seat in one of the bars or clubs. Finally we decided to give the dining room a miss but discovered there was very little in the way of optional dining in the evening: standard grills, pasta or pizza or a bit of Japanese sushi, also not vitamised. The breakfast and lunch buffets were good though so we didn't starve.

First port of call was Naples. I'd booked a private car with driver and guide for a day tour of the Amalfi Coast. And sure enough, there they were waiting for us on the pier: Antonio, the driver, and the very beautiful guide, Gabriella. We missed the famous Amalfi Coast drive last time and were so looking forward to seeing the legendary blue Mediterranean lapping the cliffs and beaches of the famous resorts and picture-postcard fishing villages.

But it fuckin' rained, didn't it? The only day of the cruise it rained and it had to be on the day we were driving the Amalfi Coast! Forget the beautiful blue Mediterranean I'd dreamed about for years, it was fuckin' grey and misty for the entire day! Okay, we still enjoyed ourselves and it was still beautiful but try pushing a wheelchair around Sorrento, Positano, Ravella or Amalfi with the rain pissing down, and trying to hold an umbrella over your wife to stop her getting pneumonia again this time.

We decided to take the manual wheelchair and leave the electric one on board as it would be too cumbersome for the sedan.
A lovely old man, a store owner, in Sorrento, thoughtfully placed a sheet of plastic over Marie's legs to keep her dry. Antonio and Gabriella were wonderful. They went to so much trouble to make up for the weather. Although it continued to rain, it gave the scenery a beautiful soft and misty look. The traffic was lighter than I expected and I was surprised that the cliff edge roads from a sedan were not as frightening as I had heard. Amalfi, even in the rain, with its multitude of tourist shops with vivid pottery and fascinating goods, was magnificent, and lunch in a hilltop restaurant in Ravella was wonderful in its misty grandeur. Rain or not, we were so glad we hadn't missed it.

Athens was the next stop.

Christos, our charming driver and guide, met us at the port of Piraeus and took us off to the Plaka for our obligatory morning cup of local coffee. The Plaka is in the old part of Athens and had been restored and designed for tourists visiting the Olympic Games. It's a lovely area with many outdoor cafes and not a sign of plastic tables and chairs for a change. Christos assured us he would provide us with the best cup of coffee in Athens. We parked and he took over as wheelchair pusher and led us to a charming outdoor café with a vine-covered trellis and comfortable padded lounge chairs. We look up at the sign over the door and, to our amusement, see it's a Starbucks! The coffee was good though and the surrounding area, very picturesque.

I had learned from the web that the Acropolis now had an elevator for the disabled. Naturally this was one of the sights we had to see so off we went intending to make that our first stop. The fuckin' traffic was horrendous and all the roads were blocked and no one was going anywhere. There must've been fifty coaches filled with camera-clicking tourists, queued up for miles. Christos suggested it might be better if we did the other sights first and come back to the Acropolis later in the day, after the tourists thinned out a bit. This we did and off we went to the Archaeological Museum, where the sculptures were astounding. then to the old Olympic stadium, where Marie remembered they'd filmed *Chariots of Fire*, but Christos was too young to remember, and finally we watched the changing of the guard, with the soldiers dressed in girlie skirts, pom-pommed shoes and funny hats.

Don't talk to me about the bloody Acropolis! It certainly had a lift to take us up most of the way but after that you're on your own. The lift was like a construction site lift the ancient Greeks had used to build the Parthenon, operated, I think, by one of the original ancient Greeks themselves. Christos told us that the guide wasn't allowed to accompany us (he was no fool), so I had to push Marie and the wheelchair up the last hundred metres or so over steep, rocky and pot-holed dirt paths, in the heat of the day. Wouldn't you think if they went to the trouble of installing a lift they'd lay down proper bloody paths?

The site was littered with rubble and exhausted tourists from all round the world, peering at heaps of rocks! I was told it is being restored and they're trying to find the original stones to go back in their original positions (?). It must be the biggest jigsaw puzzle in the world! The pollution from the millions of cars is probably destroying it faster than they can restore it.

She Who Can't Be Ignored had her usual whinge about the audacity of the British pinching the Elgin Marbles from the Parthenon and taking them back to the British Museum. At that stage I wished they'd taken the whole bloody Parthenon back and stuck it in the museum. At least the British Museum is wheelchair friendly.

One thing that really impressed me with Athens was the patience of the drivers. It's pretty well stop and start all the time and yet there was no evidence of any road rage. I suppose they're so used to it they just take it as a matter of course.

At one stage our car was blocked in a narrow lane by a van filled with a gypsy family, who calmly got out, had a conversation with a friend on the footpath, climbed back into the van and eventually drove off, without one raised, indignant voice or the honking of a single horn! I can't imagine Australian drivers being so patient, even with their Greek relatives in Melbourne.

Off across the Aegean Sea and the beautiful Greek Islands.

You had to get a tender from the ship to the island of Mykonos, the supposed gay capital of the Med, so we gave that a miss, as we didn't have the guts to run the risk of rolling off the tender and drowning, or me being propositioned, or at the very least, fondled by a hairy Greek – male or female. From the ship, Mykonos and the surrounding islands looked like someone had dumped all the rocks they'd excavated from the archaeological sites around Greece into the sea, and built a village of white boxes on the top. I suppose they were built up there as a defence against invaders. Well, it certainly stopped us from invading in a wheelchair.

Entering the Golden Horn and the magnificent view of Istanbul was breathtaking; the skyline of minarets and mosques towering over the city that spans East and West were familiar from the many pictures and films we'd seen, but unexpectedly brilliant. This was our first visit to Turkey and it is a fascinating country. Our car and guide were at the port to greet us and whisk us off for our coffee and a tour through the fabulous Topkapi Palace. The architecture and the incredible treasures will linger in our minds forever. Marie was particularly taken with the Topkapi Diamond: forty-eight carats of sparkling facets, and the other Royal jewels. She said she would've quite liked the Topkapi Diamond for an engagement ring. I told her she would never have been able to do the washing wearing it whereas the cute little one I had given her was much lighter and just perfect for housework.

We were raced through the bloody Grande Bazaar at a rate of knots, trying, but not always succeeding, to avoid the crowds of locals and tourists. I was after a leather jacket but our guide had other ideas. He, of course, had this marvellous contact outside the market who, of course, would give me a 'special deal', of course. Istanbul is famous for its leather goods and I must admit his friend's range was superb, even though he was out of stock of whips, which was disappointing. We were plied with the local firewater and nibbles and treated, as usual, like wealthy Americans. We finally made a deal and with much haggling, I finished up only paying three times what the jacket was worth. A bargain!

The big surprise with our next shore excursion in Turkey was Kusadasi, the port for Ephesus. It is actually a popular resort for the Turks and is beautiful. Our guide's name sounded like Illcare, which, as usual, I had trouble remembering, and he was positively brilliant. Our first stop, after our cup of coffee, on the waterfront of course, was the reputed Virgin Mary's house, which has generally been accepted to be genuine by at least two Popes. I've got to say it was so simple and peaceful I almost converted to Catholicism.

Ephesus in its heyday was purportedly second only to Rome in importance and grandeur. It is also where St John is supposed to have written the Book of Revelations and lived with Mary, platonically of course, until she died there.

This is the biggest test Marie has had to face so far on the trip and not a word of complaint. She is obviously fascinated with the ruins and tries to take as much in as possible.

From the web, the photographs made it look as if it was wheelchair accessible and the tour company also informed me that this was the case. In fact it is anything *but* wheelchair accessible. The main road that runs through the ancient ruined city is made of marble blocks but over the millennia the blocks have worn and broken, through the course of time and several earthquakes. The result is very rough going and once you enter, the only way out is through the exit at the other end. Illcare takes complete control of the wheelchair for the whole tour and he is amazing. He weaves, pushes, pulls, lifts and strains the whole way, hardly pausing in his commentary and drawing our attention to the various ruins.

Bloody Hell! Ephesus was no stroll through the park. The poor old love really had a tough time. She finished up with a bad case of Numb Bum. Some places were completely inaccessible for the wheelchair so she got out and, with my help, managed to limp her way around the obstacles, with Illcare in tow carrying the chair (it was the manual, not the tank, thank God) until we could find a relatively flat place where she could climb back into the chair, often with a giggle.

Illcare (or Sicko as I christened him by word association because of my difficulty remembering his name) was too busy heaving for breath to giggle. This was the sort of place you really needed to sit in the shade, only there wasn't any, and contemplate your surroundings, but we didn't have the time or the place for that luxury. Two people collapsed and one young bloke fell over and broke his leg and they were all carted off on stretchers. I thought that Sicko and I were sure to be next.

Apparently Mary and John the Apostle took nine years to walk from Jerusalem to Ephesus. Why she didn't keep the donkey and take the short cut, I'll never know.

The island of Rhodes was beautiful and we spent the day in the old town with the electric wheelchair this time, as we were still recuperating from Ephesus. It's a very touristy area but 'nice' touristy. They stop the wheeled traffic at 8:30am and leave it free for pedestrians to wander through the wonderful souvenir shops, cafes and ruins. That way you can be fleeced of your dollars without having to worry about being hit by a truck. Marie was enchanted.

The next day we arrived at Santorini, which was another tendered port so we recovered our strength on board and studied the island over several cocktails, coffee and cream cakes, and watched some of the other demented passengers scaling the cliffs on donkeys or cable car to reach the village on top only to find that the cable car doesn't return them back down the cliffs and they either have to pay for a donkey ride or walk. Is it really worth it? I mused, as I reclined in my comfortable deck chair, drinking coffee, munching cream cakes and wearing a whipped-cream moustache, with a novel on my lap. I don't think so.

Our last port of call before returning to Rome was Katakolon, a most beautiful port in Greece, and which is the gateway to Olympus. Our driver/guide, Nicholas (how unusual for a Greek), delivered us to the ancient home of the Olympics where Marie, who in her younger days dreamed of being an Olympic contender for the hundred metres sprint, was enthralled. The area around the site had recently almost been destroyed by bush fires but it didn't look as bad as I expected. The damage in Australian bush fires is much more visible. But sadly, many people had died or been made homeless by the fires and Nicholas himself had lost the majority of his olive trees in the blaze.

Because of the terrain we couldn't see much of the remains of old Olympus, but the original racing track and the museum are wonderful. Lunch at a restaurant in Katakolon beside the beautiful Mediterranean before returning to the ship, was superb. I'd never heard of Katakolon. At first I thought it was a veterinarian medical term. You know, 'My pussy had to go to hospital for a kat-a-kolon-oskopy and he couldn't walk for weeks.' Then we were told it was pronounced Ka-TAK-alon. Nowhere near as funny.

We sit on the aft deck sipping a cocktail and watch the sun set for the last time over the beautiful Mediterranean, marvelling at its size and the history it covers. It has been a wonderful, once-in-a-lifetime cruise and we are so glad we've made the effort. Sure, there have been some difficulties but nothing was insurmountable. Marie has held up brilliantly, but the pain in my hip is getting a little worse so I hope I can hold up for the final leg of our trip: the Land of the Pharaohs, our dream of a lifetime – Egypt.

Chapter 20

Fuck me! They don't wear or even fit seat belts to their vehicles. On the way from the Cairo airport to our hotel, the Meridien Pyramids, the representatives of Egypt For All, a marvellous tourist company I'd hired who specialise in assisting disabled tourists, were driving us in their van. In the evening light, I was surprised by how fascinating the bustling and sometimes beautiful Cairo looked.

About five minutes from the hotel, the driver had to hit the brakes to avoid another crazy Cairo driver and Marie, who never travels in her wheelchair in a car, rocketed out of her seat and landed splat on top of the personal assistant Egypt For All had supplied.

Hilkit was a small but wiry, English-speaking German girl who turned out to be a wonderful guide and helper for Marie, but I thought I was going to lose both of them at that moment. However, they both survived, but Marie had to spend the last couple of minutes of the journey lying on the floor of the van they'd provided, as there was no room to get her back on the seat. She was probably safer there anyway.

So we arrived at this posh hotel and slid Marie out and into her wheelchair and made a not so grand entrance up to the reception desk. Of course the disabled room I'd booked and confirmed six months prior wasn't available for the first night so, unlike my usual style, I flew into a temper tantrum and pounded my fist and heels on the polished marble floor and reception counter a few times, drowning out the loud, foreign Sufi Zikr ritual music playing in the background for a wedding celebration on the grand staircase of the foyer. The manager apologised and installed us into a suite with a view of the Pyramids for the night, promising the garden-view disabled room would be available the next morning.

The view of the Pyramids was a bit of a waste as it was night time when we arrived and in the morning, even though the Pyramids were only a couple of hundred metres away, you could barely see them for the mist and pollution.

What can one say or write about Egypt that hasn't already been seen on television, or been said or written about for hundreds of years? Well, I have to say that actually being there with the constant fascinating sights, smells and perfumes, the sounds of the muezzin *from the mosques calling the* adhan, *the call to prayer, and the unexpected friendliness of the people, record themselves in your memory forever.*

The Pyramids and the Sphinx, in the dry heat of the day or at night with a cool desert breeze wafting over you as you sit under a million stars and watch the light and sound show, are awe inspiring. The fascinating Cairo Museum with its noisy crowds and sensory overload was everything, and more, than Marie had expected. Memphis, with the incredibly beautiful, forty-five-foot reclining statue of Ramses II, the Khan El Khalili Souque, the six-hundred-

year-old bazaar with the noisy, jostling crowds shouting, laughing and haggling, are all experiences not to be missed.

How will we ever forget Thebes, the ancient capital of the upper Nile, now renamed Luxor, and the ancient temples of Karnak and Luxor, with their incredible acres of columns, decorated with finely chiselled and painted hieroglyphics, thousands of years old? To actually visit the sun-drenched Valley of the Kings and the Valley of the Queens, with tombs steeped in mystery, and a thousand gaping tourists strangely hushed by the experience, will linger in my mind forever.

Dining overlooking the River Nile, flowing peacefully through the brown desert hills with verdant shores like a bright green ribbon lining the banks, the calm flowing water dotted with colourful feluccas and passing cruise ships, and at night, ablaze with lights; this, for me, will always be synonymous with Egypt. Marie's dreams have been fulfilled.

I think She Who Can't Be Ignored spent most of her time in the Temples, and Valleys of the Kings and Queens, looking up at the sky. Egypt is not wheelchair friendly and the chair pushers were forced for much of the tour to tip the chair up on its back wheels to get over the mostly rough terrain, thus forcing Marie to lie back, almost horizontal, peering at the azure sky: Another case of Numb Bum and backache for her.

But, to their credit, the pushers persisted and where it became too difficult, there were always a couple of Egyptian strong arms to help out. Contrary to popular belief, and to what I expected, we were never hassled for *baksheesh*.

We were always with a guide, so maybe that had something to do with it. But the only time I was clipped was in an unguarded moment at the Pyramids by a souvenir peddler, who, among others, had helped Marie in the wheelchair. As soon as she was settled he approached me, pulling his wares from a shoulder bag, smiling engagingly and speaking in excellent English. Before I knew it I'd parted with twenty American dollars for an armful of rather interesting crap. He was so charming and friendly it was a pleasure to be fleeced by him. I do appreciate professionalism.

Apart from that, nearly all of the tourist stops were heavily guarded by Tourist Police who keep the local peddlers and camel keepers in line and away from vulnerable little old tourists. We cancelled a night-time light-and-sound show at Karnak Temple at short notice because we were both a bit exhausted, and found out later that the guide company had to notify the authorities that we would not be attending, as they had to have a record of where we were every minute of the time we were in Egypt. We hardly noticed the security that was obviously in place and felt quite safe the entire time we were there. I think Surfers Paradise at night is probably more dangerous and nowhere near as interesting.

My hip and leg are getting much worse and I'm limping so much the guides are not too sure who should be in the wheelchair. But I'm still on my feet and it's only a few days before we'll be home. Marie is standing up to the touring brilliantly and I am so proud of her. It certainly hasn't been easy for her but she's been having a wonderful time. Thank God I organised the help and assistance along the way.

The stopover in Dubai on the way home was 'interesting'. First of all, we landed late at night and the international airport was huge and ablaze with light like a city in itself. Emirates had landed over three hundred planes that day and the air bridges were all engaged so our plane had to park miles away from the terminal. They sent out a hydraulic lift vehicle to take the disabled passengers to the terminal.

There were seven other disabled passengers on our flight, all of them Muslim and very old and tired looking; the women in their long black robes and veils and the men, slumped and dishevelled. For a moment I thought they were all dead and they were taking us off to the morgue. It made Marie feel as though she wasn't in such bad shape after all.

Dubai is so extravagant and over the top it reminded me of a rich spoiled kid with lots of poor immigrant servants to look after him. The five-, six- and probably by now seven- or eight-star hotels and other buildings are obscene in their extravagance. The number of luxury cars speeding, seemingly uncontrolled, along the smooth bitumen roads, with obviously few road rules to restrain them, is pretty horrifying.

With a dear friend who now lives there, we enjoyed high tea at the 321-metre-high Burj Al Arab Hotel, overlooking the sea, which is dotted with man-made islands shaped like palm trees or a map of the world's continents, or something that looked like a large vagina. We then investigated the famous Gold Souk, an entire area of nothing but gold and jewellery stores where we learned that your social position depended on how much you adorned yourself with gold. Well, that put me in my lower blue-collar-class place. It was good to see where our petrol dollars were going though.

On reviewing our trip, we both agreed it had been a wonderful experience. We're both pretty proud of ourselves for managing what wasn't an easy trip under the circumstances. But secretly, I think to myself, seeing all of these exciting, romantic places is not really experiencing them. I tend not to be able to sink into the atmosphere and contemplate the world-shattering history that has taken place there, or imagine the colour and spectacle of events, or the lives of the inhabitants of long ago civilisations, while watching out for Marie's comfort and our well being.

I think one could be far better off spending time in a particular area and absorbing the culture and atmosphere rather than just seeing the sights. Maybe we'd be better off staying still, sitting in a comfortable chair with our feet up, watching the documentaries on a wide-screen television set with Hi Definition picture and Hi Fi sound. Only that way you'd miss the sights, smells and noise that surround you when you visit these exotic places. We also learned that we weren't the only ones in a similar or sometimes worse position, to take the risks and travel. But would we do it again? Probably not ... But the river cruise down the Rhine does look rather nice.

It made me realise even more how much I am responsible for Marie's well being. It is a constant worry all carers have. If something happens to the carer, what happens to the one we love and are caring for? My life is spent trying to protect Marie and to make living just a little bit easier for her. But I can do this only while I am strong and healthy.

Chapter 21

We're told there are no atheists on the battlefield. I would go a step further and say nearly all of us become devout believers when we are faced with any disaster. When every avenue has been tried and found wanting, we will inevitably turn to God. Most of us believe there has to be a higher force or energy to make sense of the suffering and torment that nearly all of us are forced to bear at some time in our lives.

But here, religion has done us a great disservice. Just going to church doesn't make you religious any more than standing in a garage makes you a BMW. The hypocrisy, guilt, lies, skulduggery, manipulation and political in-fighting in the name of God is, quite literally, beyond belief. And atheism is strictly a 'non-prophet organisation'.

However, with the decline of influence of the Church in Western society it appears that the mantle of religious fervour has now fallen on the shoulders of the Celebrity thanks to the efforts of overpaid Publicity Agents in league with the persuasive power of the rampant Media who will gladly fill their pages and our television screens with any sort of crap. It appears that mankind needs a belief in something to revere but I don't think a teenage pop star, a film or television star, a Lance Armstrong or other drugged-up sports star or a boy band is going in the right direction for moral, ethical, or spiritual beatification. God help us.

Most religions are based on either a loving God or a vengeful God, depending on your persuasion. Over the centuries, missionaries have been sent into foreign countries to convert the natives to a foreign-based religion and inevitably to destroy their culture, all in the name of their God. We have one of the most powerful religions in the world run by a dictator and his henchmen who wear gold- and silver-embroidered dresses and funny hats. (Hardly an image of Christ on Earth.) And these same men instruct their disciples on what to believe, how to behave and think. Come on, guys, this is the twenty-first century; may I suggest a white mini-skirt, grubby white runners, a baseball cap worn, of course, backwards, and a white T-shirt with the words emblazoned across the front: For Christ's Sake, Get a Life! If you have bad legs you could go for a below-the-knee skirt if you're sensitive. In winter it could change to a grey trackie, to save on the laundry bills, the same grubby runners, a black woollen beanie, and the words Get Your Ecstasy From God! stencilled on the back of the jacket.

The fundamentalists of another powerful religion, who also wear funny tea-towels on their heads, or veils to cover up their bad acne, are not condemned and excommunicated by their leaders for allowing their faith to be used as an excuse to send men, women and small children as suicide bombers to blow themselves and innocent bystanders to smithereens, all in the name of Allah.

Both of these religions are supposedly based on a loving and just God and yet, despite the horrors they inflict, religions persist. If the Vatican was an oil-producing country, I'm sure the Americans would find an excuse to invade. If we are to believe in the loving, personal God of the preachers, it makes little sense of the natural world and certainly the societies in which we live.

Most religions are based on a God figure or image, and the teachings of a prophet who got the word on a direct line from the Almighty. We have been conditioned to pray to this entity and assured by the religious leaders and philosophers that our prayers will be answered. And if they are not, then it is our fault because of our lack of faith or incorrect manner of praying or hundreds of other reasons, or because, when all else fails, 'God works in mysterious ways'. You can say that again!

But it is inevitably our fault, never the all-knowing religious leaders or their Omnipotent One. The religious leaders are well schooled. They have had hundreds or thousands of years of study and contemplation, manipulation and brain-washing to explain the reasons or excuses why your faith has failed you, and none are satisfying or justifiable to an intelligent person. Because, in the end, regardless of their claims, all the religious leaders are human, and therefore fallible, and over the centuries, much has been lost in re-telling, translation and interpretation.

From ages of old we have been led to believe that there is an Omnipotent Magician who waves his staff, makes everything all right, and creates miracles for the worthy, and only a select few have direct access to him and to the true meaning of his teachings.

What a crock of shit. Certainly, read and contemplate teachings and philosophies, but literally, for God's sake, and yours, make up your own mind. Frankly, I have a natural suspicion of any prophet, religious leader or teacher who spends forty days and forty nights wandering the wilderness, without food or water to sustain them, and then suddenly having an instant revelation and communication with their God and being told, 'This is the way, the only way. Go forth and teach thy brethren', or any other like advertising slogan.

Now excuse me, but in that condition, wouldn't you think their brains could be a bit addled from food and water deprivation, and isn't it just possible they could be hearing things or suffering some brain damage from their ordeal? I'm sick of hearing of so many nutters who have a direct line to God and who convince so many desperate people they will be 'saved' if they follow their particular path. With the cost of calls, how can these 'Friends of God' afford their mobile bills?

If you have a taste for Religion, is it a Cardinal sin to eat a Bishop or a missionary?

Some years ago I happened to log on to a website which included an audio interview with a self-proclaimed Pastor of some American, (wouldn't ya know?) fundamentalist, evangelical nut farm, who is also on direct speaking terms with God. He had been instructed to warn the world – that is of course, the Americans – that the end of the world would definitely begin in April 2008. Nuclear war and natural disasters would combine to cause the destruction of the world in a very nasty way. There would be no escape and nowhere in the world would be spared unless you believed in this religious nutter.

The problem was he sounded so rational and convincing. I didn't believe a word of it of course, but just to be on the safe side I sold all my shares to fill the petrol tank, packed up the wok and a bag of rice, filled a ten-litre plastic bottle with water, threw some clothes and undies in a suitcase, readied the over-toilet seat, bed post, drugs and prescriptions, checked the credit cards and washed She Who Can't Be Ignored's hair, and waited. I was also instructed by you-know-who to pack the mongrel cat into the pet pack. I resisted, of course, saying there wouldn't be room in the Camry for my guitar, but she insisted. Oh well, we could always use him to flavour the rice I suppose.

When it got to June and there was no evidence of an imminent Armageddon, I had a growing suspicion that God had changed his mind yet again, so unpacked everything – except the cat, who I placed out on the footpath with a For Sale sign attached to his cage. No takers, so I had to bring him back in again. Further proof there is no God like the one they told us about. And I determined never to join a religious cult; I prefer to practise safe sects.

It is rather sad to see thousands of people crying and praying to their God to save them from disaster and some are saved, and others suffer a terrible fate. And those who are saved then offer up their prayer of thanks for being spared. What about the other poor bastards that didn't make it? Who decides who will be saved? God? That doesn't sound like a loving God to me. Do the ones who are saved always deserve it? Evidence proves otherwise.

Now in the West, India is presented as a very spiritual nation and thousands of people, and rock stars, flock there to find spiritual fulfilment. This is a popular misconception promoted by the West and bears little resemblance to the true situation. It's true that you can find yourself armpit deep in Gods and Gurus. The interesting thing is that you can choose the Guru that is right for you. If you decide that you really want to be filthy rich and drive a Mercedes, and be waist-deep in virgins in the next life, and not give a damn for the lower castes, you search around for a Guru that will 'enlighten' you to get the things you want, and if he won't, you dice him and shop around until you find one that will. The Hindus have literally hundreds of gods to worship and pray to, so take your choice. The one good thing is belief and religious doctrine does give a lot of people comfort of a sort and keeps them off the streets. – Not in India, of course.

Also in India, it is not unusual for elderly men to renounce their wealth, wives and family and retire to the mountains for solitude and peace, which I guess is understandable, to meditate and contemplate the mysteries of their lives and hopefully discover enlightenment. I notice this is not so acceptable for women as no doubt they are required to keep an eye on the children and grandchildren, oversee the cooking and cleaning, and continue their God-given right to give advice and interfere. Now, for a man, this is a good thing because at that age you are no longer really relevant to society as a whole and it's a good time to reflect and prepare yourself for the final adventure.

Now I'm a bit of an Indian myself but in my situation I cannot really piss off to live alone in the mountains or the bush, because I have certain responsibilities and self-imposed duties, which are important to me. I can, however, retire to the mountains of my mind and wander the paths of my existence.

These paths may be rocky and mostly uphill, but it is a fascinating journey. I have tried to follow these paths for most of my adult life; reading and studying religions and philosophies, normal and paranormal and scientific findings, and I find that I have now come to certain, if not absolute, convictions.

First of all, what if we call God, say, Doris or Tom? 'A rose by any other name.' What if God, Doris, or Tom, is really an intelligent power or energy source that runs the Universe? Okay, so science tells us that it all began with a Big Bang but who or what set off the bang, I want to know? Obviously it is Energy, or Doris or Tom, which after all creates matter. But maybe matter isn't the all-important thing.

They've spent billions of dollars on the Large Haddon Collider in Switzerland to discover what happened after the Big Bang. Who gives a shit? Surely the billions could have been better spent helping to solve the world's food crisis, or in providing medical care for Third World countries, or any other number of tangible problems. Most of us don't give a damn where we came from, we care more about the here and now or where we're going.

What if we are souls or sparks of this source energy that has always existed, and choose to travel through what we know as time, space and different dimensions to gather and absorb experiences? What if Doris or Tom, through natural selection or attraction and rejection, created the basic building blocks of this beautiful physical planet for us to experience as part of our development and evolution took over until a suitable body evolved for our souls to inhabit? And what if we chose to come here to gain the knowledge we needed for our development? And what if we are free to make our own Karma, choices and decisions and reap the results, pleasant or unpleasant? And what if, at the end of this existence, through natural death from illness or degeneration of matter, or accident, or war, or physical abuse, we cast off this physical body like a suit of clothes and our soul moves on to another dimension to continue our journey?

There have been scientific tests that indicate that the body inexplicably loses a couple of ounces of weight at the point of death, not caused by the loss of fluids or air or any other perceivable matter. Could that perhaps be caused by the release of the soul? Other reputable tests have been done with Near-Death Experiences, Clairvoyance, Spiritualism and hundreds of other so-called paranormal sciences, the number of which are astounding and in many cases, as verifiable as possible by reliable witnesses.

And yet, many people will refute and denigrate these beliefs without prior investigation, their minds tightly closed to any possibility that they could play a very important part in our very existence. Maybe this knowledge or interest is not a required part of their development this time around in this life plan. But even if we find one scientifically verified example of the evidence of the soul and what is called paranormal activity, it must change the world's way of thinking and behaving. Surely we'd be nicer knowing that we are responsible for our lives in this dimension and do something about it while we're here.

Chapter 22

For my part, I had an experience that, in a very important way, helped to shape the outlook I have today. It was in Melbourne in 1972. My wife and I had been married for twelve years and, because of Marie's irregular or lack of ovulation, we had been told by every specialist we visited that it would be very unlikely that we would conceive a child; this was despite a new fertility drug treatment which had failed three times and almost caused her to have a nervous breakdown.

We had put the thought of ever having a child out of our heads and in part, it was the reason we decided to move to Melbourne to try our luck in the acting profession. We both shared an interest in what was then considered the occult, esoteric or paranormal, certainly not to any extreme but purely as an interest in being open to ideas.

Because of this shared interest, we visited an acknowledged, reputable psychic who lived a couple of doors away from the Police Station in South Yarra, which was pushing things seeing as charging for clairvoyant readings was then against the law. She was a delightfully funny and vivacious blonde woman, probably in her early forties, who greeted us warmly and ushered us into her living room.

Without preamble she invited Marie into her 'Reading Room', and closed the door behind them whilst I leafed through a magazine. I occasionally heard their voices through the door, punctuated with much laughing and giggling. After about half an hour, the door opened and Marie was escorted back into the living room, wearing a somewhat puzzled smile, and without further delay I was invited in for my 'reading.'

I sat down opposite the clairvoyant at a table and she asked for my watch or wedding ring to hold while she spoke, saying it helped her pick up my vibrations. I must say I was somewhat sceptical and on the lookout for any chicanery, unwilling to say anything that may give her any clues. This didn't seem to bother her in the least and she began.

After a long pause she told me that I was an actor – well, although I was not what you'd call over-exposed, it was possible she had seen me on stage or had heard of me, or Marie had mentioned it. She then went on about my work, which was very spasmodic at the time, and said that I would soon be very busy and in demand and that no matter what, I was to accept everything that was offered and somehow it would all fit in to place.

She mentioned a television company I would work for that had a large 'C' in the title, and another television show for the ABC, the producer of which she didn't like the feel of much and warned me about, and other stage and radio work that would be rolling in. If only this is going to come true, I thought dubiously, it's going to be worth the twenty bucks.

She then hesitated and said, 'I can see you and your wife planning to go overseas soon.'

This was actually true, as we had decided to do the 'Grand Tour' of Europe that was so fashionable with actors at that time and try out for theatre work in England. In fact, we were planning to purchase our tickets the following week, but I thought my wife may have mentioned that to her as well.

Then she said, 'I'm sorry, but you won't be going on that trip for quite a while.' She paused again and said, 'Look, your wife laughed at me but I can definitely see a baby boy coming for you and your wife next June!'

This was early in November at the time and I chuckled and said, 'No wonder she laughed, that would mean (a quick count of the fingers) that she's already pregnant.'

'Yes, I suppose it would,' she said. 'Well, I'm sorry, but I'm definitely getting a baby boy arriving in June. And it will be a Caesarean birth.'

At that stage I thought, well, there goes my twenty bucks; another well-meaning phoney. Shame, I was so looking forward to all that work she'd predicted.

I really didn't take much notice of what she said after that, having made up my mind she was, at best, well-intentioned, if a little off the mark, and we left. On the way home in the car, we compared notes and had a good laugh about the evening.

Over the next few months offers of work came flooding in: television, stage and radio, including a contract with Crawford Productions which had a large 'C' in their logo, and a second contract for the ABC for the television series, *Bellbird*, with a producer, as it eventuated, who was exactly as she'd described him. Work became as hectic as she had predicted. Despite some hassles, I was able to fit everything in including an offer for stage work that I had refused three times because of my television commitments. The production company insisted they wanted me for the role to play opposite the wonderful Australian star of Musical Comedy, Jill Perryman, and went to a lot of trouble to change rehearsals to fit in with my television commitment; something virtually unheard-of in those days for a relatively unknown actor.

But the biggest surprise was yet to come. A few weeks after the reading my wife came home from work one evening and calmly announced that she had killed a toad. As she was always one for the slightly off-beat remarks, I replied, 'Oh, that's nice, dear. Did you use the four iron or the putter?'

'No, I killed a toad!' she replied, somewhat a little too stridently, I felt. I looked at her, somewhat puzzled, wondering where this fascinating bit of trivia was leading. After a suitable pause she almost screamed, 'I'm pregnant!'

I have no definite complete recollection of my response but I think I fainted.

In those days there were none of those packets you could pick up at the chemist, whip into the bathroom and Bob's your uncle, or maybe, the father. They used to do a pathology test, which involved injecting the woman's urine into a toad. If the toad died, you were pregnant. How's that for advanced technology? The toad was literally 'pissed off' and I don't blame him. Well, unbeknown to me, my darling wife had started to realise a couple of weeks after our visit to the clairvoyant that she was feeling a bit tired during the day and often dropped off to sleep for a few minutes whenever she got the chance, which was very unlike her. She also noticed she was visiting the toilet much more often than usual, which was also very unlike her normal habits.

Although they were her only symptoms, she'd remembered that they were sometimes symptoms of pregnancy and that, together with the prediction, unknown to me, she was secretly enticed to make an appointment with her gynaecologist to check it out. Following the bombshell announcement, she made another appointment with her gynaecologist, and after confirming the pregnancy, he told her it would have to be a Caesarean or neither she nor the baby would survive. 'I know,' she told the gyno, 'the clairvoyant told me.'

He did the classic double take and said, 'Oh, I see, and do you have any idea when the baby will be due?'

'Well, the clairvoyant told me it will be in June and it will be a boy.'

To his credit he smiled, albeit condescendingly, and said, 'Well, I think she might be wrong. By my examination, I think it will be May.'

'Okay,' she said, 'we'll see who the better fortune teller is, shall we?'

Over the following months the pregnancy went very smoothly with Marie growing bigger and more beautiful until we reached the beginning of May. The gynaecologist was a very ethical type and said he wouldn't do the Caesarean until the baby was ready, so obviously he wasn't a golfer. This was in the days before ultrasound so this meant we had to present a urine sample to the Pathology Department at the hospital every second day until the baby was 'ripe', as he put it.

So every second morning, armed with a bottle of pee, off I would go to the hospital. The urine would be tested and they would phone us later in the day with the result. This went on right through May with no positive result and into June until eventually on the 27th June, the gynaecologist rang to say, 'Okay, we have lift off, you'll go into hospital tomorrow and we'll do the Caesarean that evening.' According to the X-rays, our son, as we were by then convinced it would be, refused to turn down into the birthing position and was blithely sitting upright with his legs crossed and his thumb in his mouth, looking like he was waiting for a bus.

In those days fathers weren't allowed into the operating theatre for the birth, which I thought was a very good idea, being a habitual fainter, so we missed the comedy/panic one was led to expect of pre-birth ritual and instead, calmly packed the suitcase, shampooed the hair, checked the tyres on the Volkswagen, arranged the oxygen for me in case I fainted, and set off for the movies, to sit and watch *Godspell*. It was all very controlled and peaceful.

The next day I delivered Marie to the hospital and went off to work, telling her I would return later in the afternoon. By the time I returned she'd been prepped for the operation and we were both very excited and a little tearful, facing this momentous occasion in our lives which we never imagined would ever happen. Then came the endless waiting and corridor-pacing in a cloud of cigarette smoke. Of course those were the days when you were allowed to smoke in the waiting rooms, which was very calming and civilised.

At about seven-thirty I saw this medical orderly coming toward me pushing a trolley that looked like it had a plastic cheese cover on top. He smiled as he approached and said, 'Mr Williams? I'd like to introduce you to your new son.' He lifted the cheese cover and there was the most beautiful, perfect baby I had ever seen. And he still is.

This remarkable psychic's name was Shey Berryman and understandably we became quite close friends. I heard from other sources that it was considered that she had an eighty percent success rate with her readings. All I know is we had intriguing success with her over the following years. She was prone to ring me on the phone and say, 'I've got some hot tips for you.' On one particular occasion she predicted three deaths that I would hear of. This was very unusual as it was the only time in all the years I knew her that she ever predicted a death and to hear of three in one phone message was a trifle disconcerting.

The first was the death of a family member, an older man but not my father, she said, from interstate, which I would hear about by what was then called an STD phone call. Today that would've meant he'd died of the clap or some such sexually transmitted disease I suppose, but it those days it was the name given to an interstate phone call. She also said I would be worried about the health of an aunt. After a couple of minutes of general chat she suddenly said, 'Oops, there's another one. Another older man – a relative – not your father – also from interstate.' Again we chatted and suddenly again she said, 'I don't believe it. There's another one. That's three separate deaths! The third one is also an elderly man but he's overseas and he's just a friend or acquaintance. Sorry about that.'

Within a week I received a phone call from my father in Queensland telling me that an uncle had died of a heart attack, running into a telegraph pole while driving his car and his wife, who was sitting in the passenger seat without a seat belt, had been thrown through the windscreen and was seriously injured in hospital. A short time later I received another call from Queensland telling me another uncle had died in Canberra, and a few weeks later I heard of the death of an old actor friend in New Zealand whom I had directed in a television series called *The Box*. I said to Shey, 'Okay, enough with the death predictions. The next one might be mine and I'd rather keep it as a surprise.'

A few years later my wife woke me in the morning to tell me that she'd just had a telephone call from a friend to say that Shey had suddenly died the day before. Apparently she had died from pneumonia and probably wouldn't have died if someone had sent for a doctor, but they mistakenly thought that as she was so 'spiritual' she would be able to heal herself. I was performing in a stage show at the time and that evening my understudy had to take over my role as I completely lost my voice from shock.

The friendship was an intriguing experience and although it encouraged me to open my mind to possibilities, it also made me realise the great danger that can exist from ignorance and misunderstanding the power of the Universe. The ability to make predictions may be interesting but the outcome must never be taken as inevitable or one hundred percent accurate or allowed to interfere with your decisions. Our free will overrides all else.

I have had to take the words 'quickly' and 'hurry' out of my vocabulary. She can only move very slowly and everywhere we walk together I am clamped to her left side like a limpet or a suckerfish, ready to steady her in case she stumbles and falls. She's had a couple of falls and it's very difficult getting her back on her feet or to a chair.

She must hate being so dependent; I know I do, not for the extra work but the extra responsibility. Taking care of her is my sole job now and the world we knew is changing every day and passing us by.

Chapter 23

Now with this theory of soul continuance: it is also quite possible that some altruistic souls, who are only too aware of the difficulties we face here on Earth, may choose to stay in contact with the so-called living to help them with support and guidance, when genuinely needed. Maybe they can only make contact when our minds are at rest or peaceful and not clogged up with distractions. Maybe our brains are both receivers and transmitters and when we throw the switch we open up the channels of communication between dimensions. Maybe the departed find it difficult to lower their vibration rate to match the grossness of ours.

Maybe these communications aren't always seemingly reliable and maybe the monkey chatter of our minds distorts or blocks the message. But I have found that, in extreme conditions, when I inwardly plead for help or direction, within a short time, sometimes without realising it, my mood lifts and I see things in my mind much more clearly, and within time, a course of action will be presented to me. I have the choice to make the decision to accept or reject it. I have been following this practice for quite some time now and the results have been extraordinary.

It only seems to help with a mood shift or an opportunity that will open up for me. I never seem to get a response to a specific request for personal gain because what we pray for may not be what we need. All I can say is, I do get a positive strength and a lighter mood to continue to cope and this is invaluable.

Because we humans seem to require a name or a face to communicate with I feel uncomfortable calling the source 'Angels', as it seems a bit implausible or childishly romantic, owing to the connotation of heavenly beings with big white wings flapping about in an airless environment and the connotation instilled in us by early religious teachers and artists, as beautiful as they may appear in the old paintings and sculptures. I think they were meant as symbols to satisfy the culture and spiritual needs of the time.

And so, in my mind, I simply refer to my source as Soul Friends or Spooks and ask them to lighten my mood and give me a bit of advice to overcome any particular problem I'm having.

And when the reply comes, which it inevitably does, I always thank them when they come up with the goods. The rest is up to me. They provide the inspiration but it's my job to actually follow it through. Maybe it's in my imagination or maybe I'm linking up with Doris or Tom. Or maybe, after all, it's only my subconscious working on my requests and presenting the solution. Who knows? If it works, don't question it.

If my grand theory of soul continuity and Reincarnation were proved to be true, think of the benefits to mankind. Euthanasia would no longer be looked on as a crime and it would take away the fear and mystery of death and we would see it as just another step along the path of our soul development. Pain and suffering would have purpose. Perceived problems would have a point, a chance for us to learn and overcome, and maybe we would become more tolerant and compassionate, and understand why people act the way they do, because we are all on a different journey, a different level of development; not better, but different. Justice may have a more truthful meaning.

Maybe we could even bring back the mandatory death sentence for the inhuman lowlife who have made the wrong decision, who torture, rape, plunder and murder the weak, vulnerable, and innocent; the perpetrators of genocide, the generals, politicians and terrorists who invade with force and destroy precious life experience, opportunity to develop, and freedom. If people can't live within the borders of decency and common humanity, give the world a break and get rid of them. Send them on to their next dimension for re-education. But isn't the death sentence just another form of savagery?

I am not a great believer in fate, as it is commonly thought of, and I know God or Doris or Tom or my higher self won't give me more than I can handle, but there are times when I just wish they didn't trust me quite so much. I'm more inclined to believe that our fate is probably a likely outcome from our and others' thoughts, actions, decisions and choices we make, and have made, along the way. Shey may have had success in her predictions for us but I believe we could've changed the outcome if we'd chosen to take another path to the one we were on. Time and synchronicity are strange bedfellows. After all, we judge time mostly by birth, seasons, degeneration, and death. It's a much larger and more esoteric subject and maybe only Doris or Tom has the answer.

My philosophy seems to work for me. It may change. That's why I say I'm 'almost convinced', because I'll never actually know until I come to the end of this journey. But if I'm wrong and there is no soul continuance, then I'll never know anyway, will I? It doesn't completely do away with pain, despair, sadness and suffering because they are mainly human emotional attributes created in our brain, but it makes things a little easier to understand along the way.

I can just picture the Philistines out there, sneering and shaking their heads at my naivety as they sip their beer or Chardonnay and crunch their potato crisps. Well, these are my thoughts, my experiences, this is my journey, and this is my life, so if you don't like it, bugger off.

There is so much we are unable to do now; like simply taking a walk on the beach as we were so fond of doing, or fishing in the surf at sundown with the crystal-clear water and the white foam swirling around our legs, and the miraculous sky changing colours as the gold-red sun sinks below the horizon, colouring the clouds in glowing pinks and blues and mauve, playing golf or tennis together, walking through the bush and inhaling the scents of nature, or strolling through the shops. So many other simple things we took for granted are now no longer possible. We now have to find less energetic pastimes and although we are restricted, there is much more time for living in our hearts. May Doris or Tom give us the strength to carry on.

Chapter 24

Now I'm not exactly a climate change sceptic and the available research from the majority of scientists seems to have merit but the arguments and debate on man's effect on climate change and global warming rage on. Al Gore suddenly emerges from the mists of political ostracism as the Messiah of Global Warming and Climate Change! Lo and behold, and wouldn't you guess, this has now become a multi-billion-dollar industry with the ever-increasing number of interests vying for their cut. Well after all, that is America, the land of opportunity, the land of disjointed Democracy, and the land of the Sub Prime Mortgage debacle.

It looks like those in favour of the global change argument, with their billions of dollars for scientific research at stake, have made substantial gains over those against. Governments all over the world, who unfortunately rule the masses with never-ending fear campaigns, are coming into line and heeling to the popular press and media and hence public opinion. And we all know how much we love a good disaster and doomsday story. It appears to me that newspapers, popular media and alarmists present only the science that supports warming because it's more sensational. I remember in the sixties, global *cooling* was predicted and we were heading for another Ice Age. Let's get together on this, guys.

From, I admit, my limited research, it would appear that there are considerable questions concerning the argument that man's activities are entirely responsible for global warming, and that it is possible some of the damage could be a product of natural cyclical orbital mechanics and solar variability among other things. For a start it is generally accepted by scientists that the Earth was considerably warmer in the time of the dinosaurs, with the CO_2 levels two to four times greater than today, probably due to the huge amount of farting going on and the volcanic activity, I suppose. The huge amounts of methane gas being farted into the atmosphere by animals, and some of the more flatulent oldies, is horrifying. When I was young I was always told it was 'not nice' to fart in public and to hold them in. This was very dangerous because if you hold them in they travel up your spine to your brain and give you shitty ideas.

Why don't they make it a law for every business and private residence to be responsible for its own solar power supply? Maybe we could fit big bags or canisters over the asses of the world and convert it to power our cars and run our power stations. There are a couple of blokes I know at the Retirement Resort who could power a fleet of buses. Simplistic, I suppose, but maybe very effective.

The projected temperature rise seems unrealistic when you consider that global temperatures have risen by a little over one degree over the last one hundred or one hundred and fifty years, during the height of industrial expansion. This is considered by many reputable scientists to be a trivial amount in the natural variation of the Earth's temperature and very sustainable.

Also, as regards oil spills, what about the millions of litres of oil that was spilled out of the thousands of ships that were sunk, or planes that were shot down over the oceans during the Second World War? The oceans recovered in time. Give nature a break and it will repair itself. But we do have to help it along so for God's sake let's clean up our act. With today's technology, coal-fired power stations can be cleaned up so why do we sell coal to dirty power stations? I now learn that greenhouse gases are the highest they have been in 800,000 years. How do they know that? Were they higher 800,000 years ago? I'm pretty old but I can't remember that.

One must also take into consideration the issues of changes in calibrations and measurement protocols, urban heat island issues and the placement and design of temperature stations. A lot of the global warming predictions are done on computer modelling, which is not infallible.

Of course we should clean up the atmosphere, oceans and waterways. Of course we should stop cutting down all the trees. Of course we should use alternative energy sources; if not for ecological reasons, but for the huge effects on the living standards and economies of the world. Of course we must recycle. But if we didn't have so much unnecessary plastic packaging and junk mail we wouldn't have as much to recycle, would we? I'll get more serious about recycling when China and India stop buying our coal, until it's clean, or they stop building coal-fired power stations altogether. Let America and the rest of the world get together and stop the reliance on coal and oil. Go on, upset the multi-national companies if you dare, or if it's possible. Go on, rattle the chains of the Middle East. If we're really serious we've got to go for the big guns.

To begin with, how about the capitalist world starting to pay the poor people of South America, New Guinea and any other Third World country not to cut down and burn the rainforests, which absorb more carbon monoxide than any other technological development. It's called Carbon Emission Trading, folks. If we need carbon emissions for our gluttonous way of life, which is affecting world weather and maybe global warming, then the gluttons have to pay for it. We can't expect poor, overpopulated countries not to clear and burn the rainforests and go hungry for our sake. It's not only that the forests and ecology they support are pretty; it's an economical and life-enforcing necessity!

It's not all that straightforward, and at my age, hardly worth getting my knickers in a knot about. Like most of us 'Little People' or 'Battlers', or whatever the current term is today for those just trying to get by, I, like the majority of the world's population, have many more immediate, pressing, day-to-day issues to contend with. I hardly think being forced to separate my garbage, and turning off a couple of light bulbs, and only flushing after a big job is going to save the planet.

God I feel awful. I really lost it again the other night. It's not her fault, it's the situation. But the reason doesn't make any difference. She's in such a helpless position, always having to rely on me for the slightest thing. It must be terrible having to put up with my frustration, impatience and sense of inadequacy as well. I've got to keep reminding myself that no matter how tough things are for me, she's in a much worse place. I've got to be there as her lifeline.

Chapter 25

The week we returned from our trip, the stock market crashed – sorry, I mean, had a 'correction'. I can imagine all of the financial institutions in the world emailing each other saying, 'Oops, we've been giving all the little shareholders too much money. And we need that money to pay the millions of dollars in retirement bonuses and outrageous salaries for our shifty CEOs who helped us lose the money in the first place. We'd better "correct" that. We'll sell a squillion shares at the high prices, and that will bring the market down and give us a humungous profit, and then we can buy the shares back at the low price, so when they climb again we can sell them again and make another huge profit. And what's more, we don't even have to pay for the shares up front. It's a fucking gold mine!'

Then we had another few 'corrections', that sounded for all the world like a crash to me, and bang went millions of dollars of our superannuation that we were forced to invest in by Government regulations in the first place. And we were responsible? Now, just when you get to the stage you can manage to make ends meet, they move the fuckin' ends!

The avaricious banks and financial institutions gave loans on houses, or cars, or trips, or probably even for my mongrel cat's vet bills if I'd asked, without checking to see if they were able to be repaid. I remember when we used to go for a loan, we had to provide endless documentation and suffer undignified interviews which stripped bare our psyche, to prove that we could afford to pay it back. We didn't have an endless amount of credit available on an endless number of credit cards from an endless number of shysters.

These days if you want to buy a house, these same banks and financial institutions are offering a huge percent of what the house is worth on today's market. Look what happens when the market dropps. Don't ask me to feel sorry for those poor stupid bastards who lost their million dollar houses in the infamous Sub Prime debacle to buy rental properties to rent out at exorbitant prices to tenants who couldn't afford to buy a house of their own because they were paying such high rent. You really only need one house to live in, you know. And if you can't afford the fucking mortgage repayments, then don't take out the fuckin' mortgage! If you don't know by now that the market goes up and down like a shagging stallion, then you're too bloody stupid to buy a house in the first place, let alone a second one.

I saw yet another supposed sob story on one of those ghastly current affairs programs on television the other night, complete with the obligatory tears of course, where some silly bitch had lost two multi-million-dollar houses! And now the poor old dear has to live in her year-old Mercedes Benz! 'And it's so hard to start over again at my age,' she wailed. Tough luck lady! You should've known not to gamble on the wonderful 'self-regulated' market.

Don't you just love that term? Don't make rules and regulations to control the greedy bastards, who are a natural part of humanity; trust them and the market to do the best for you and they'll 'regulate' themselves, and screw you as you deserve to be screwed.

How different it used to be. Sometimes we had to strip off and have a medical examination to make sure we wouldn't get sick or die before we paid off a loan. Mind you, that was with our bank manager, whom I suspect was a bit of a pervert. Why else would he require a prostate check in his office?

'Now, while you're undressed, would you bend over the desk, Mr Williams, and I'll just check your assets.' And this was with him standing behind me, with both of his hands on my shoulders. Hmmm, funny that. I got the loan though. So you see we got shagged one way or another in those days too.

I visit two Specialists and a Physiotherapist before they finally discover my left hip replacement has in fact loosened and will have to be replaced. No wonder I was in so much pain. Thank God I survived the trip.

Now I have to worry about what to do with Marie while I'm in hospital and recovering. I won't be able to look after her! What I have feared has suddenly come to pass.

Through a Respite Care organisation I manage to finally get her into a new nursing home, miles away from the hospital where I'll be having my operation, and miles from our villa, friends and family. I know she's going to hate it. The home and the surroundings are quite pleasant and our wonderful neighbours are incredibly helpful, driving us everywhere and shopping for us, because I can't drive in my condition.

Chapter 26

When She Who Can't Be Ignored worked as an Administrator in a wonderful Melbourne-based hostel and nursing home for the aged, I have to say she was brilliant in her job and the staff and inmates adored her. She used to go to so much trouble with menus and nutrition and activities and genuinely cared about the comfort and welfare of the old dears. Our home became a catering kitchen for fetes and fund-raising schemes. Many was the time she conned her staff members into a production line of cakes, sausage rolls and pasties, pickles and jams, to be sold at their annual fete, to raise money for equipment that would not be funded by the government.

One of the essentials she always provided for the workers was several casks of wine. I, of course, would escape to a worker-free zone, only to return later to a bunch of drunken pastry cooks flinging ingredients and cooking utensils around the kitchen in wild abandon, chattering and giggling hysterically. She organised raffles for dolls, dressed in beautiful costumes, all designed and sewn on her ancient Singer sewing machine. There was nothing she would not turn her hand to.

There were the funny times when she told me of some poor old thing whom she would find standing in the hallway of the hostel, with a suitcase at her feet. When asked the perfectly natural question as to what she was doing there, the old lady would reply, 'I'm just waiting for the bus, dear.' Or another one standing alone in the hall would say, 'Mrs Williams, somebody just peed down my leg.'

Another one would strip off all her clothes and go walkabout and the police would ring and say, 'We've got Mavis here in reception again. Would you come and get her? And bring a coat to cover her; we're getting a lot of complaints from the local street gang.'

Another old guy would ring for the nurse to show her, with great pride, the huge erection he had managed to achieve. Another old lady was dying and the doctor kept upping the morphine dose to ease her pain. She took to it like manna from heaven and survived happily for months. The larger the dose, the better she got. She died with a smile on her face.

She is very brave and appears to accept the situation even though I know she's frightened and loathing the prospect of our separation. The night before my operation when I have my own natural concerns, she rings me from the nursing home, almost in tears, and says, 'I can't stand this. I'm going to check myself out and go back home. I'll be able to look after myself.' She can't, of course and she doesn't check out. But I do break out in nervous cold sores.

To the strains of the surgeon singing the Bee Gees' 'How Do You Mend a Broken Hip', I am placed on the operating table and, lulled by the gentle background sound of a waiting electric buzz saw, drift into oblivion, dreaming of a time when there are no leg braces to put on and take off twenty times a day and no wheelchair to lift in and out of the back of the car, and my wife, having dressed all by herself, running free, waving both arms in the air and then embracing me in love and joy.

The operation is a success and for the first time in months I have no pain, even though I am not given any pain-killing drugs. Not that I would've objected because I really got off on the Pethidine they gave me last time. My blood pressure had dropped, as it always does when I have an operation, but I was so happy, I couldn't have cared less. This time, no happy drugs, bugger it, and no secret fags in the bathroom, blowing the smoke out the little window and quietly singing Leslie Gore's hit 'It's My Procedure and I'll Smoke if I Want To', and getting sprung by a nurse who was counter-singing Helen Reddy's 'I Am Woman Hear Me Roar'. It was sort of like an opera or a concert version of excerpts from Broadway musicals.

This time they got me up on my feet and pretty soon I was almost sprinting along the corridors on my crutches. The saintly neighbours brought She Who Can't Be Ignored up for a visit a couple of times which was great, and I was able to convince her that I wasn't screwing the nurses as she suspected because my blood pressure was too low to even get a rise for the sexy, sixty-year-old Red Cross magazine lady who came to call.

We keep in contact constantly with our mobile phones and commiserate with each other. After about a week, I'm told that I will be going into rehabilitation for a while until they can arrange for my Home Transitional Care. The rehab hospital turns out to be the Very Dreary Old People's Nursing Home I spoke of earlier. The care by the staff is excellent though and the food is what one imagines is the typical mush old people are forced to eat. I lose four kilos in weight while I am in there and almost go into a mental meltdown. Marie and I talk often on the phone every day comparing situations. Her food is prepared by a Chinese 'chef' and she is offered either a Western cuisine or Chinese. Coming from North Queensland originally, she had many Chinese friends who were excellent cooks and consequently, loves Chinese food, so decides on the Chinese menu.

Well, the chef's idea of Chinese cuisine was anything that had rice on the plate. You could have pie and peas but as long as it had rice with it, it was Chinese. His other specialty was canned baked beans, which is also a well-known Asian delicacy of course. For several days they had baked beans on everything and apparently the place smelled like there was a leak in the gas pipe. The pièce de résistance was that other traditional Chinese fare, spaghetti with canned baked beans sauce. Now, She Who Can't Be Ignored is a little finicky about her food I'll admit, but for some reason she simply couldn't face the sight of baked beans, with their orange-coloured runny sauce, oozing over a plate of Irish/Chinese stew with mash, and of course, rice.

Because the home had only been open a short while and wasn't at capacity accommodation level, they didn't separate the different grades of care in the dining room, so she could find herself sitting opposite, or next to, a poor old Alzheimer's case who shouted obscenities to the rest of the room while peeing down his, or anyone else's, leg, while the sweet old lady adjacent farted in time to her munching.

I think the nurses and carers who work in nursing homes should be paid a few thousand dollars a week, which of course they aren't, because they certainly deserve it. Mostly, they are brilliant in their patience and kindness. My experience was nowhere near as bad as Marie's because at least I could get up and walk away to my ashtray in the garden. Marie's nursing home was a completely non-smoking facility of course, because they didn't want these poor frail old darlings dying now, did they?

At last I was gratefully released from incarceration and returned home. Transitional Care nurses, Physiotherapists, Dieticians and housekeeping staff invaded a couple of times a day to take care of me. Marie was not covered by Transitional Care, as she was not the recovering patient despite the fact that I was her sole carer, so we had to enlist the help of another agency to call on her to help her shower and dress and set her up in her recliner for the day. The whole process was incredibly helpful and appreciated of course, but the reliance on strangers and invasion of our privacy was hard to take.

Chapter 27

I really don't think of myself as a 'carer'. I think of myself more as a wife-looker-afterer. I remember getting a hell of a shock when I was allocated a Carer Pension; that was, up until I the day I turned sixty-five and it instantly turned into an Old Age Pension. Did that mean I was no longer a carer?

When I see or hear of the real carers, the ones who have young or old children or parents, some unable to move, or bathe themselves, or toilet themselves, or who require constant medication and nursing, my heart goes out to them. What happens to the young carers who have a family or a career and a mortgage and still have to pay for equipment, medicines and the many other expenses out of the meagre income they receive? How do they survive financially? How do they survive emotionally?

How can I consider myself a carer when I don't have the worries of maintaining a career; when I receive a Government Pension to augment my savings; when our son has grown up into a self-supporting adult; when my wife is able to communicate and get out of her chair and walk short distances? It made me think of the foreign countries we'd visited which appeared to have little or no assistance for the old, frail and disabled, and made me appreciate the country we live in. We saw very few native Turks or Egyptians in wheelchairs on our trip. In Istanbul or Cairo I didn't see one person in a wheelchair or even on crutches and yet they must exist.

One wonders how on earth they survive and get around in those overcrowded cities where the underprivileged are the majority. Perhaps they don't. The terrible picture this brings to mind is truly horrifying.

How do the disabled cope in the outlying remote areas of the world where life is simply a matter of survival? How do they survive? Why do they want to? Do they have a choice? Why do we desperately cling on to life when there's little chance or hope of improvement? If my spiritual theory is true, it seems we are all on our different journeys and at different stages of development requiring different stimulation, and that is why we see such diversity in life, such conflict: the advantaged and disadvantaged; the mega rich and the dirt poor; the loving and the evil; the healthy and diseased; the strong and disabled. It's all in the journey, I suppose.

The lessons are hard but maybe it is our soul, our link to the Universe, pushing us on, knowing that at the end of this journey there will be revelation and peace before we choose to return, with no conscious memory of our last journey to influence us. Or maybe we move on to another dimension, and yet another and another, for even further development until, at last, we become at one with the Universe, to play our part in Creation.

There is obviously an order in Nature; why should there not be an order for mankind? Unlike the plants and animals of the world, we have imagination; we create art, music and poetry. We rise above instinct and we reason. We use advanced mathematics and science. We suddenly receive inspiration that transcends our usual thought patterns. To me, it indicates a higher, more complex intellect that surpasses the role of evolution of matter. Maybe the brain is more of a receiver than a transmitter after all.

My heart cries for her as she awkwardly gets out of her recliner and makes her way, very slowly with the aid of her walking stick, to the bathroom. The transformation from the lithe, energetic lady I married is almost unrecognisable.
 'You need any help?' I ask.
 'No, I can manage, thank you,' she replies.
 But to be on the safe side I station myself at her left elbow as usual, ready to steady her if she happens to stumble which happens from time to time.
 She tries to be very independent and I try not to discourage her. She so misses her independence and the ability to be able to look after me and our home like a 'normal' person, as she puts it. This is the greatest sadness of all.
 Later we sit on the back deck with a cup of coffee and chat while we look out over 'the swamp'.
 'You know,' she says, 'we have a pretty good life under the circumstances, don't we?'
 I look at this beautiful, crippled old lady sitting opposite me, this shade of the woman she was and smile, fighting back the tears.
 'Yep, pretty good for old pensioners,' I reply, as I make my way back inside ostensibly to get her another piece of cake as an excuse to have another good cry.

Chapter 28

In the meantime we just have to put up with the injustices, like unnecessary, hermetically sealed plastic packaging that requires a chainsaw to release the vacuum-packed goods inside; prefabricated furniture that requires a degree in engineering to assemble; television, computers, and all the other frustrating technological equipment we must have, that need a five-year course at a university to program and understand. And why must I pay over ninety dollars for a pair of jeans, faded, frayed, crumpled and torn, that look ten years old? That's what I'm wearing at the moment. I want a pair that looks new, for God's sake! Why should I iron wrinkly clothes? I don't iron my body.

Single-ply toilet paper! Now there's another ploy by the manufacturers to make you use eight times more. Otherwise you have to clean your nails more often. When I was a kid, we used torn up newspaper, and when we really wanted to impress visitors, it used to be cut into nice little neat squares and tied into bundles, with a bit of string at one corner and hung on a nail. The print used to come off on your bum so you got real skid marks on your underpants, I mean like an FJ Holden with locked brakes on bitumen. My grandmother was very posh: she had proper rolls of real toilet paper! Oh, the luxury of visiting her.

Or what about graffiti that hideously disfigures any public surface that stands still for a minute, or fire alarms that go off and give you a heart attack whenever you burn the toast? Spare me the sight of those beautiful young athletes with their glowing youth and strength, who fortunately can't even contemplate the ravages of old age.

And, for heaven's sake, let's not forget the cynical, whining, pain-in-the-ass, grumpy old men who cannot face the fact that their youth and relevance is over, and spend their time resisting change, and regretting the opportunities they missed or let slip by. The list goes on and on. You show me someone of my age who has no regrets and I'll show you a bad case of raging senility..

When I look back on the more perfidious areas of this incarnation, I must admit I do emit the occasional high-pitched, hysterical giggle. But when I do, I always subtly check to see no one is watching. I swear I've noticed a big white van occasionally stalking me and on the side is a sign which reads, 'End of the Road Hospice for the Elderly Disturbed'.

I'm not being paranoid, just careful.

Chapter 29

Marie's father, Archie, was a musician. Archibald was the rebellious son of an English surgeon and his wife, the beautiful Olive Mary Harriman, who died at a very young age of consumption. Their father, distraught from the loss of his young wife, and completely neglecting his two young sons, shot through from Blackpool to a little mining village by the name of Troi D'Rui near Merthyr Tydfil in Wales and gained distinction for his medical work in the mines.

Archie was packed off to boarding school at the tender age of five, where he developed a strong disgust for mutton in any shape or form. His only brother, Patrick, was killed in a motorbike accident at the age of twenty-one.

On finishing boarding school, Archie fled to Milan in Italy to study music as he refused to follow in the footsteps of his father and, as the elder son, take his expected place in the medical profession. It was also rumoured he fled to escape the stern, philandering father who was having a fling with the local dentist's wife, which came to a sudden *coitus interruptus* when the dentist came home unexpectedly and shots were fired.

We only found out many years later when we visited the village in Wales where her grandfather had practised – surgery, I mean, not dental implanting – and the legend had lived on. Father and son never communicated with one another again.

After gaining his honours degree in music, the tall, slim, long-haired, blonde young Archie eventually found his way to Genoa and via Egypt to Australia by working as a member of the band on a cruise ship out of Alexandria in Egypt, which, in the late twenties, was rife with terrorists. (How times change!) In a very unlikely scenario, he made his way to Ipswich in Queensland, of all places, and met and married Doris Mary Winifred Clegg, who became infatuated with the handsome, sophisticated young English musician. Well, there wasn't a lot of culture in Ipswich in those days and tall, handsome, long-haired, blonde Englishmen weren't actually thick on the ground.

There certainly wasn't enough work for a musician, so what to do to support a wife and young family? Move to Edmonton in Far North Queensland, of course, and become a cane cutter. That's how desperate some people were to get out of Ipswich. They eventually moved into Cairns where they lived in a tiny, four-roomed house, and Archie joined the Army and was shipped out to New Guinea, where he played in the Army band and shot the odd Jap, I suppose.

Cairns was the place where Marie discovered the joys of living in the tropics with pale skin, in a house that backed onto a swamp that tended to flood in the wet season, bringing a vast array of wildlife into the overgrown backyard and outdoor dunny. Archie later bought a full-sized grand piano from the departing American troops and installed it in one of the four rooms of the house, thus rendering the already tiny room utterly useless for any other activity.

A few years after the war, Archie moved the family to Brisbane, an absolute Mecca after living in Cairns, where he was appointed head of the Woodwind Department at the Queensland Conservatorium, and where he was very highly regarded. Marie was drop-dead gorgeous and took to the sophisticated city life immediately and this soon brought her to the attention of an equally gorgeous, tall, dark, handsome, young, hopeful, would-be actor whom she eventually married and twelve years later, bore him a son. So you can see it wasn't exactly a shotgun wedding.

After nearly fifty years together, the now plain, grumpy, grey-haired, limping old ex-actor finally moved her to a villa in a 'Retirement Resort for the Over Fifties' which backs onto a swamp! How the wheel of life turns. Although, to be eco and politically correct, in the brochure it is referred to as 'Natural Vegetation Wetland', which, when you come down to it, is a fuckin' swamp, as She Who Knows a Fuckin' Swamp When She Sees One refers to it.

Chapter 30

The Conclusion
March 2014

'Now remember,' I said, ' if you need to use the commode, wake me up so I can help you out and back into bed, okay?'

'I managed last night,' she said, 'I don't want to disturb your sleep.'

'But you aren't used to this bedroom,' I stressed. 'I don't mind being woken up for that. I'd rather you wake me than find you flat on the floor, okay?'

We were spending a few days at my sister and brother-in-law's apartment on peaceful Bribie Island, just north of Brisbane. We'd had a lovely relaxing time, reading, eating out, sightseeing, night fishing from the pier and sitting, with wine glass in hand, on the front deck looking out over the beautiful and serene Pumicestone Passage that separated the island from the mainland.

At 3.00am I was awoken by her calling my name. Alarmed, I bolted upright and turned to face the other side of the bed to find it unoccupied.

'Where are you?' I replied, somewhat still confused from my sleep.

'I'm down here on the floor,' she replied, rather subdued.

'Fuck!' I scrambled out of bed and hurried to her side on the floor at the foot of the bed, 'Why the hell didn't you call me like you said you would? Are you alright?' Worriedly I quickly checked her over to see if there was any serious damage.

'I think I might have sprained my ankle and my bum's a bit sore. I slipped on the new carpet.'

Concerned, I helped her to her feet and back into bed but she had trouble bearing her weight which she could usually manage reasonably well.

She'd had a few other falls in the past but she was always capable of being helped up and transferred to a seat or bed. I chastised her for being silly not to wake me but she replied she was fine but just a bit sore.

'I'll be right tomorrow,' she assured me. 'Give us your lips and go back to sleep, pretty boy,' her usual goodnight request. 'Sorry if I frightened you.'

The next day she was understandably still shaken and sore so she rested as much as she could but she was still having trouble weight bearing, which we put down to perhaps spraining her ankle. I decided it would be best to return home and visit our usual doctor so I packed the luggage, helped her to dress and we left.

The doctor checked her for any possible fracture of her ankle, knee and hip but even though he could not find any fracture, he sent her for X-rays to confirm his prognosis of a sprained ankle. The X-rays confirmed his diagnosis and her ankle strapped and we returned home to recuperate.

Two days later the pain and weakness had increased to the extent that I took her to the hospital where they admitted her for observation and further X-rays and Cat Scans.

The results showed that she had fractured her pelvis. She was prescribed strong medication for her severe pain which eventually sent her into a semi-comatose state.

The nightmare began.

Because she was unable to stand and bear any exercise or physiotherapy, her lungs became infected and she sank further into a coma and was moved into Intensive Care. The next day I was called into the attending doctor's surgery.

'I'm sorry, Mr Williams, I'm afraid the prognosis is not good. She has developed pneumonia and is not responding. In any case, because of her age and general condition, it would take many months for the fracture to mend and even if it did I doubt if she would ever return to even her previous strength or capability.'

My mind could not or would not accept the prognosis. She had always been such a fighter. But the realisation of his following words shocked me into gut-wrenching sobs that tore at my inner being. 'I think we're going to lose her within the next forty-eight hours.'

The almost unbearable vigil began with friends, some flying in from interstate, and relatives visiting to pay their respects and say goodbye. She was very well loved. Our son sat with me at her bedside and played and sang her favourite songs from his childhood on his guitar. We talked to her but she seldom responded to our company. And any words she uttered were mainly unintelligible.

Inevitably, at 9.00pm on the 3rd April, I received the phone call from the hospital. I was at home, where I had returned to shower and change. I had not been with her at the end. Maybe that was how she wanted it. Dying is such a personal thing.

My grief smothered me like a cold, wet blanket. The culmination of fifty-three years of marriage and fourteen years of sadness had finally arrived and I joined the countless number of others who have visited and departed this Earth who have been forced to confront their suffering, mortality, loss and grief: lives lived in pain and sadness with small windows of joy and happiness to keep us going on to complete our life plan.

Now was the time when my beliefs in the soul and the afterlife would be tested to the extreme.

Chapter 31

Fortunately we had discussed our demise and funerals previously when the time seemed so far away and we could afford to be flippant. Others who are forced to attend to the arrangements need no words from me to explain as each person's grief and pain are unique. I hate to read about the five stages of grief, which didn't pertain to me, as it is so general and clinical and I loathe being a statistic. We each had decided the ceremony should be a simple, joyful recognition of our lives but Marie claimed for my funeral she would borrow a black riderless horse, trailing a tie-dyed tee shirt and board shorts-draped casket for my procession. She would place my empty thongs, or flip flops, reversed in the stirrups and borrow her brother's two .22 calibre rifles for a two-gun salute. The cortege of mourners hired if necessary, would be dressed in hippy garb and sing 'Let the Sunshine In'. So glad I didn't go first.

An extract from the eulogy I gave over her beautiful, pink rose-painted casket is an indication of the admiration, respect, loss and love I experienced on that day.

> *'Yes, I am grieving but I have been grieving for the last fourteen long years since Marie suffered that devastating stroke which left only the shell of the vibrant, funny, energetic, laughing Marie I married and we all knew so well. A friend once remarked Marie was the only person he knew who actually laughed in musical arpeggios.*

Unfortunately that laugh and much of her vibrant personality disappeared with the stroke.

She hated going to funerals but I guess this is one she couldn't avoid. I'm sure she would've if she had a choice but it was the end of this journey for her and time to move on to her next adventure in the afterlife.

When she attended anybody's funeral she always sat in the back row and invariably sobbed and cried very loudly even when she hardly knew the departed. Many were the suspicious looks that were shot at her from grieving widows who immediately suspected she must've been their departed husband's secret mistress. 'Who is this beautifully dressed and groomed blonde grieving so loudly for my late husband?' they would wonder. Let's face it she was an emotional mess at funerals so please, no tears today.

On a serious note though, Marie and I have an unshakable belief in the afterlife and the continuing journey of the soul, which is a great comfort to me at this time despite the awful sadness, and I know she is with us today in spirit unfettered by pain and paralysis that plagued her last fourteen years so I hope I don't hear her uncontrollable weeping and sobbing from the back of the chapel as it would embarrass us both.

Marie was what is now considered an old-fashioned wife who devoted her entire life to our marriage, to Ben and to me. Yes, she was an extraordinary woman and she taught me many things in the 53 years we were together. I never quite succeeded in equalling her as a cook or housekeeper in her eyes but the most important lesson she taught me, friends, was, unquestionably, unconditional love. She unfailingly supported me in any endeavour I undertook and, let's face it, in the world of stage and television, some of them were pretty hairy, and she would stridently and forcefully defend me and our son against any criticism, which I admit in some cases, although very few, may have been justified.

So I look forward to joining you in our next adventure, my love, and there are so many stories I intend to relate in my next book which is tentatively entitled, A Light at the End, which, with my other seven novels, will also be available on Amazon at very reasonable prices.'

Never miss the chance for shameless self-promotion, she would say.

Chapter 32

Like many people who lose their loved ones, I continue to talk to Marie as if she is still physically present. It's hard to overcome a 53-year habit. Unfortunately, she never seems to respond but a couple of strange things have happened.

A few weeks after Marie passed, I was sitting in my chair in front of the television, about 9.00pm, involved in a relatively interesting program on Foxtel and not thinking of Marie at all. Suddenly I heard her voice calling me very loudly, not in my mind but in my ear!

'Yoo hoo …'

My skin turned to ice and I jumped up from my chair. It was such a distinctive call which she used often to attract my attention when I was in a different room and she needed my assistance.

Immediately dismissing the notion of a visitation, I hurried to open the front door telling myself I was imagining things and it was just my neighbour calling out to me. There was nobody there and no one to be seen in the vicinity. I quickly checked the other doors and windows to no avail. I called out her name but there was no further response.

I'd also had a couple of seemingly inexplicable things occur like my son reporting a dream he had of his mother standing in the kitchen of our previous home, looking much younger and completely recovered, saying, 'I'm alright now, I just needed a big sleep.'

I realised this could well be a product of his imagination or wishful thinking but it did lend itself to things I had read about past life encounters with souls who have to endure a ' big sleep' to recuperate from a severe and lasting medical condition or trauma they had suffered on Earth.

Then there was an acquaintance who certainly didn't consider she had any psychic ability, who reluctantly emailed me that although she'd only met Marie once or twice, she'd had a vivid dream of Marie saying that trying to get through to her (the acquaintance) was like talking to a brick wall, a familiar phrase of Marie's.

I had also sworn I heard Marie whisper 'Bryonnie' (a favourite name she often called me) in my ear one night shortly after she passed while I was again sitting in my chair watching television, but immediately dismissed it as a trick of my imagination. Similarly, I also attributed to imagination a loud rhythmic rapping noise on the wall that woke me from a deep sleep one night, which I immediately thought was an intruder but on investigation was unresolved. My overhead kitchen lights flickering and dimming and then returning to full brightness from time to time but finding no power problems with other lights could be explained by electrical interference.

As you will by now realise I have a strong interest in Parapsychology and the paranormal and they are subjects which I have researched and studied for most of my adult life. I and many scientists and physicists accept that the conservation of energy is an absolute law even though it seems to fly in the face of things we observe every day. Energy cannot be destroyed or dissipated but it can be and is provably transformed. We are energy clothed in matter and I believe our energy is transformed at death of the physical body and we move on as individual entities into other dimensions for other experiences for eternal soul development.

Western scientists are also beginning to accept that the brain and the mind are actually two separate entities. It appears they are discovering that the brain is a biological receiver and transmitter which receives and transmits material and information from an independent mind. Shall we call the mind an aspect of the soul?

As C.G. Jung commented, 'I shall not commit to the fashionable stupidity of regarding everything I cannot explain as a fraud'.

Attitudes are constantly changing in mainstream physics as interest in inter-dimensional phenomena becomes more acceptable and accessible to the scientific world. A very interesting paranormal investigation, The Scole Experiment, witnessed by several distinguished scientists, was carried out in the late nineties by a group of psychics and reputable witnesses in the Norfolk village of Scole in the UK and later demonstrated in the US and many other foreign countries, which was very evidential in suggesting the possibility and likelihood of inter-dimensional contact.

Reincarnation, although widely accepted for thousands of years in Eastern philosophies and religions and over half the world's population, is not generally recognised in Western civilisation or culture but there has always been constant interest. There is an enormous amount of scientific information available on what is termed the Paranormal. There has been excellent research done on the subject of reincarnation, for instance, as evidenced by such respected scientists as Dr Ian Stevenson and Jim Tucker from the University of Virginia, Dept of Psychiatry and Neurobehavioral Studies, and many others.

Fascinating research on NDE from scientists such as Dr Kubler-Ross and Dr Bruce Greyson, and parapsychology investigators from the Rhine Research Centre, Durham N.C., and many other accredited scientists and researchers, continues to be carried out but the Western mainstream chooses to ignore this vital information which could bring much consolation to unsatisfied or questioning minds. Perhaps there's no money in it?

So what does it mean to me? Past and future lives as claimed in the reincarnation theory give me a complete explanation into the vagaries of life as we know it without the need to blame it on a God figure or to dismiss it as pure accident or coincidence. It puts more responsibility on the individual and our right of free will. It explains the seeming and obvious inequalities, relationships, the reason for suffering, and the sense and need for compassion and, most of all, the power of love.

This belief does not eradicate my sadness and the dreadful sense of loss that always lies just below the surface but it does help to put it into an acceptable perspective and for that I am grateful.

Religion, ritual and doctrine which has been distorted by power, interpretation and the need to control, has been largely abandoned by the educated and free thinkers of the world as they desperately search for answers in their hearts. For example, Geoffrey Robertson

QC claims that the commonly accepted interpretation of the Islamic tenet of martyrs being rewarded in Heaven with seventy-two virgins is misinterpreted, the accurate translation being seventy-two RAISINS. This would explain the number of fruitcakes who are committed to extremist terrorism.

Like many grieving spouses and people who have lost their loved ones, and with my personal beliefs, my need to confirm Marie's continued existence in some other dimension became almost an obsession. Research into survival of the soul became almost my exclusive interest and source of intellectual study as I delved further and further into the mysteries of our existence.

With growing interest I was intrigued by the amount of similarities in supposed reports of the Afterlife by respected past life regression hypnotherapists such as Dolores Cannon and Michael Newton and many others. The evidence based on thousands of case histories was too consistent to ignore. Dolores Cannon's book on Jesus and the Essenes gave me an understanding of Jesus far more believable, logical and understandable in this age than the Biblical version. Cannon claims that Jesus was a very highly developed soul who chose to reincarnate at a particularly difficult time in man's evolution to show a misguided civilisation 'The Way', which was the name given to his teachings by his disciples and the early Christians. It is claimed by the many reports I have read that when the world becomes dangerously infected by negativity, highly developed Watchers incarnate on Earth to assist mankind to overcome the evil that men do and guide them back onto 'The Way'. Perhaps that helps to explain how despite superior force, and against all likelihood, Hitler, Stalin, Pol Pot and many other tyrants through history were eventually defeated by the righteous. But the belief also states that not all reincarnating highly developed souls arrive as religious or influential leaders but many reincarnate as simple ordinary people to encourage those they come in contact with to withstand negative energy and continue the fight. But man is, some say, cursed by free will and continues to push the boundaries of greed and the power to control their fellow man so the battle will always continue.

Michael Newton's *Journey of Souls*, and *Destiny of Souls*, agreed remarkably with Cannon's and many other therapists' description of the Afterlife gained through clients' past lives and between-life experiences. Could this be a vast conspiracy to deceive and defraud? I don't believe so. Are they there for the serious searcher to contemplate the evidence and conclude that maybe there is a 'light at the end of the tunnel?'

Remembering the success we had had with the remarkable psychic Shey Berriman, in Melbourne in the early seventies, a couple of months after Marie's death, I sought out a local psychic who had been recommended to me, hoping for some confirmation of my beliefs. She was a very kind and likeable elderly lady who had many years of psychic experience to her credit. Unfortunately I was disappointed with the reading as she was unable to describe the image Marie was projecting or give me any acceptable confirmation that she was in fact in contact with Marie's soul or spirit. Apologising for her failure she explained that many souls who had experienced trauma or difficult health problems before passing went into a state she described as 'a big sleep' while their soul was being healed and restored. To her credit she did not charge me for the second unsuccessful visit.

However, nine months after Marie's passing I attended another session with a different psychic who I learned ran the local Spiritual discussion group. This was much more successful as without prompting she described the image Marie was projecting and her personality to a tee. She described her as looking about forty years old with a good, ample but not fat, figure, fair, clear complexion, streaked blonde fuzzy hair that curled around her face, and which Marie kept arranging just so (a habit Marie certainly had), an infectious laugh with a very bright personality and sense of humour. She topped it off with the statement that Marie was wearing bright colours and *orange high-heeled shoes.* At last Marie had got back into the bright colours and high heels she loved so much.

But where most of the reports I'd read about passing over were described as peaceful and smooth, Marie's description was somewhat different. She stated through the medium that she did not want to die and couldn't understand why the doctors couldn't treat a simple fracture of her pelvis. She had told the doctors in some of her last lucid moments that she didn't want to die. She related through the medium that she didn't want to leave Ben and me and she believed there was so much more for us to enjoy in this life and she was very sad we didn't have the chance to say goodbye properly. 'They just kept upping the drugs,' she complained through the medium. This of course was true and the source of much grief for me at the time. Because of her comatose state the doctors were never able to explain to her the fatal prognosis that had developed.

She claimed that she had been met and assisted with her passing by a wonderful loving being and that she was met by family and friends who had passed over. She also informed me that she had not resolved the problems with her father and mother but it wasn't all that important as just because they had passed over didn't necessarily mean that personalities changed drastically. It was more of an acceptance without blame of the situations they had experienced in their past life and lives that had made them respond as they had.

It appears it took a lot of healing and counselling on the other side before acceptance could take place. Marie had a stubborn streak which she recognised and which it appears she took over to the other side. Unlike many reports I have read, she didn't describe any review of her past life with a council of elders as such but she did describe a sort of list of her achievements and non-achievements she had set herself in her life plan that she 'ticked off', saying that, on the whole, she hadn't done too bad a job this time around.

Now with even more reason I needed to confirm my belief in the continuance of the personality after physical death and continued with my studies on the subject and this eventually led me to Amanda, a very reputable medium with an impressive reputation. I had never met or heard of this lady before and made a booking for a face-to-face reading. She appeared as a very normal, pleasant and charming lady, aged I would say in her early forties. As she led me into the room where the reading was to take place she told me not to say anything to her until the reading was in progress and I could then ask questions if I wanted at the appropriate time but I was not to provide any information. There was a short pause as we settled comfortably into our seats and she switched on her CD recording equipment. After another short pause she closed her eyes for a few moments and the reading began.

The first thing she said was that there was a crowd of spirits around me who were eager to communicate but soon the focus fell on my wife who she said had passed over. I asked for confirmation expecting a description of Marie as I had remembered her. But the only description she could give was that Marie appeared to her as a globe of energy emitting coloured lights. Amanda explained that she was in contact with the essence of Marie and not a physical form as such. This was in keeping with other accounts I had read but I wanted confirmation.

'She's smoking,' Amanda announced with a smile. 'I hate the smell of cigarettes,' she laughed. 'Oh, thank you love,' she continued. 'She flicked it away and apologised and said she had given smoking away now but wanted to verify to you that it was her coming through.'

Marie was a heavy smoker, particularly in her later years, and claimed it steadied her nerves. Although I tried to restrict the number of cigarettes she smoked it was a constant battle.

'You gave her two wedding rings, she tells me, many years apart. She was sorry she couldn't keep wearing the first one as it meant so much to her. The first ring was engraved in a different colour, or was it a diamond? The second one was plainer gold band but she loved them both.'

Marie's fingers swelled after the stroke and she could no longer wear her original wedding ring which was a gold ring with an engraved band of white gold. We renewed our vows the year after she suffered the stroke in a lovely but poignant ceremony at our home with friends and family and I presented her with a new engraved, plain gold wedding ring which she wore till her death.

'She's so glad you kept her special dress, she's saying. She didn't mind you getting rid of all the other clothes but she's glad you kept that dress.'

This puzzled me as I thought I'd given all of her clothes to charity and it wasn't until I got home and was cleaning out the wardrobe in the second bedroom the following day that I discovered Marie's wedding dress which we had wrapped up and placed in a plastic bag on the back of a shelf. This was indeed a special dress.

She related how we'd met at a party and what she'd said when she first laid eyes on me: 'He's mine. I'm going to have that one', which the reader will recognise from earlier in this book. She also correctly related how she'd developed an aneurysm, bleeding in the brain, which led to the stroke, and becoming disabled and being entirely dependent on me and falling face down off a chair which eventually led to her physical death. She hated leaving Ben and me but it was her time to go. She knows I felt bad about not being with her at the end but assured me she had actually left her body earlier when Ben and I were sitting with her and Ben was playing his guitar for her. 'Besides,' she said, 'I came into that body alone and wanted to leave it on my own.'

At first I was a little disappointed with the reading as I didn't feel I got the information I was expecting or hoping for but apparently that's not how it works. It wasn't until I replayed the CD recording the next day and noted down the valid points that I realised that out of the hour recording, there were at least twenty-four points that were highly applicable. They included her strained relationship with her father and that she was still too frightened to talk to him on the other side in case he hadn't changed. She referred to her English grandmother, my father and mother who were among the spirits who greeted her on the other side and that my father said he worked on boats. He actually owned a fishing boat business in Caloundra after the war. She also truthfully related about my son's personal problems and how she loved him so much and was trying to help him. She saw that I had recently repainted the inside of our villa and it was much brighter (I had it painted in a pale custard shade only a few days before the reading) and I'd changed the floor. (I had a wood laminate floor laid over the white tiles just before the repainting.) That it was her birthday (three days before the reading but she always insisted on celebrating her birthday for at least a week). She also mentioned that she watched me writing a book about our life together. (I started writing this book in its current form about six months prior to the spiritual reading.)

And most importantly that we had shared many lifetimes as lovers and this certainly wasn't the last of them and when it was my time to go she would be there, holding out her hand to me and leading me back into the Light.

On reflection, I am now convinced of the validity of my beliefs and although I still and will probably always miss Marie terribly in her physical form I have found a certain contentment and reassurance knowing her spirit and personality goes on and our bond continues. It feels more like she's just gone away to live in a different country but will still keep in touch.

Marie's mind remained sharp, thank God, during the last years of her ordeal and she retained her sense of humour, which helped us both to continue to lead a mostly contented life and inspired her to sit on the back deck and put pen to paper to give expression to her free verse, poetic inclinations which now follow.

Aside from that, she always insisted on having the last word and this novel will be no exception.

Till we meet again for our next adventure, my love, thank you for sharing this life with me.

LIFE ON THE SWAMP

Sixty years ago, I swore I'd never live on a swamp again,
But this is now, and that was then.
This swamp doesn't spill all over the nearby ground.
Not a monsoon to be found.
That far away, long ago swamp behaved until the rains came
And flooded our entire property,
From the back fence to the front.
I loathed it.
 I took it as a personal affront.

In the midst of the pool that was our backyard, sat the outside dunny.
To a small child, the nightly trek through snake-infested waters to this inconvenience was decidedly unfunny.
As I stood on the top step staring at the black lake, I was told
'Off you go, you'll be good as gold'
No friendly light showed the way.
No loving hand led the way.
Every time the long grass brushed against me, my mind shrieked 'SNAKE'!
My little self would quake.
NOT GOOD.

I recall Mum at the family wash as dirty water and insect litter
Swirled around her knees.
No wonder we were prone to the odd tropical disease.

Mum became very bitter.
As did the horse egesting in the backyard.
Of course Pop got the blame.
His solution –he piled us all on a train and to Brisbane we came.
Not the horse, of course.

THE BIRDS

The birds are out in force to-day.
The ducks lining the pond start to play
Behind them range the magpie geese,
Like a squad of police
On traffic duty.
The scene is one of tranquil beauty.

Tall and white, the heron stands on the mound,
While black waterfowl mill around.
In single file, the plovers stride the path.
Two adults and two chicks,
Tiny puff balls on the end of match sticks.

The ibis ambles over looking for food.
Never seen a bird so unclean.
I give my usual lecture on personal hygiene.
It's for his own good,
But he heeds not a word.
You are a truly disgusting bird.
Go take a bath.

Does the ibis have a reason to be?
None that I can see.
I have seen them clean the odd trashcan.
A job better left to a man.
A man doesn't dive in head first and emerge covered with dirt,
Sorry if your feelings are hurt.

Rocky sits in a patch of sun,
Quietly watching the birds having fun.
I hold him back
Lest he have a mad inclination to attack.
You never know how a cat
Is going to react.
In a nearby tree, some birds sing gaily.
I hear them daily.
I hear them, but I never see them.
The peace is shattered,
When stroppy and loud,
The crows arrive in a mean black cloud.
The plovers pretend this hasn't mattered,
But the adults fall in beside the chicks
To prevent any nasty crow tricks.
Does the crow have a 'reason to be'?
Tell me.

POOR PUSSYCAT

Have you looked out back to-day?
The sky is no longer grey
The sun shines warm and bright.
Spring has sprung over night.
The trees have burst into fresh new leaf.
The vibrant pink is a stunning relief.

Some trees have golden tips, some have red.
A splash of colour along the whole garden bed.
The scarlet bottlebrush is out in full flush.
Behind them, the mangroves look a bit dead.
The trunks and branches still bare and grey
While the canopy is lush green overhead
Further away, dark and stark, some gum trees rise against the clear blue skies.
This wondrous bushland sight
Fills my Aussie heart with delight.

Rocky peers out at the scene.
I doubt he even sees the green.
From what I understand
A cat's vision is rather bland.
Many shades of grey,
Shapes only, no colours, the experts say.
How very sad is that,
Poor, poor pussy cat.

PAINFUL LOVE

Oh, Rocky, you're being such a pest.
It really hurts when you walk across my chest.
I am not some public thoroughfare,
Just an old lady in her chair.
Try walking on the floor
That's what it's for.
A woman could take offence
Finding her bosoms covered in pussy dents.
On your bike, Rocky
Take a hike.

AIN'T NATURE GREAT?

Good morrow, my sweeting,
Can you hear the birdies tweeting?
They sit in tree yonder
Singing so merrily
What a delight to hear
They bring joy to my ear.
What about you?
Do you feel joy too? You do?
Ain't nature great?

COCKATOOS

Hey, Rock, have you noticed how much cockatoos chatter?
They really make a clatter
They natter away non-stop
Whether from treetop
Or en masse from the air
They simply don't care for the sensibilities of others
Be it human or be it bird.
No one can get in a word
For their incessant conversation.
This is my personal summation.
You are vastly pretty.
Your noise a ghastly pity.
Please fly away elsewhere,
Maybe to Lake Eyre.
No one will care
That you're loud and intrusive there.

THE UNWELCOME VISITOR

On our veranda, this morning, sat one smug cat,
The problem was that,
It was not our pussy cat.
Ours was inside, shouting abuse, so angry, his small frame shook.
'Well, well, Marcel,' I said.
Then the intruder fled.
That's all it took.

Rocky was inclined to give chase,
If only to save face.
But decided instead
To go back to bed.
He really was most offended,
Probably more than Marcel intended.
He's been in a flap all day.
His fur has turned quite grey.
He won't forget any time soon.
He's outside now, baying at the moon.
'Go to hell, Marcel.'

CAT NUMBER ONE

Oh Rock, you are so cute.
Nobody would dispute
That you are cat number one
As you sit in the sun.
Such beauty of color and form
Show you are not the cat norm.
I'd back you if I were a punter
Medici Crocodile Hunter.

A MOTHER'S ADVICE

Oh Rocky, please
Don't fling yourself so heavily when you roll.
It will take a terrible toll.
You'll get arthritis in your elbows and knees.
I have warned you but you forget
You'll have to visit the vet.
He'll give you shots to heal your pain.
Please don't do it again.
I thought you'd understand.
It is for your own good.
Please take my advice
And just think twice.

GET ORF!

Good morning Rocky, my cat
Are you getting fat?
On my lap you weigh a ton
Go sit in the sun.
Enjoy your time outside
You sit on me all day, once we move inside.
You're fonder than a new bride.
There's nowhere I can hide.
I love you too,
You know I do,
But I don't sit on you at every chance

And leave fur all over you pants.
Use some discretion
In your displays of affection.
Is it affection?
Or do you merely seek a warm soft spot?
The latter as likely as not.

MORNING PRETTY BOY

'Morning pretty boy',
Caught the attention of both
Husband and cat.
Must remember that.
Cat smiled
Husband looked a trifle coy.
How could I tell
A little flattery went down so well.
Cat started to play
And I make my husband's day.
I must tell them this more often
If just to see their demeanour soften.
Husband is an absolute gem
The very best of them.
Husbands that is.

– Marie Williams

www.ingramcontent.com/pod-product-compliance
Lightning Source LLC
Chambersburg PA
CBHW071907290426
44110CB00013B/1315